ADVANCED COMPUTER NETWORK

SECOND EDITION

PROF. RAHENAAZ PATHAN

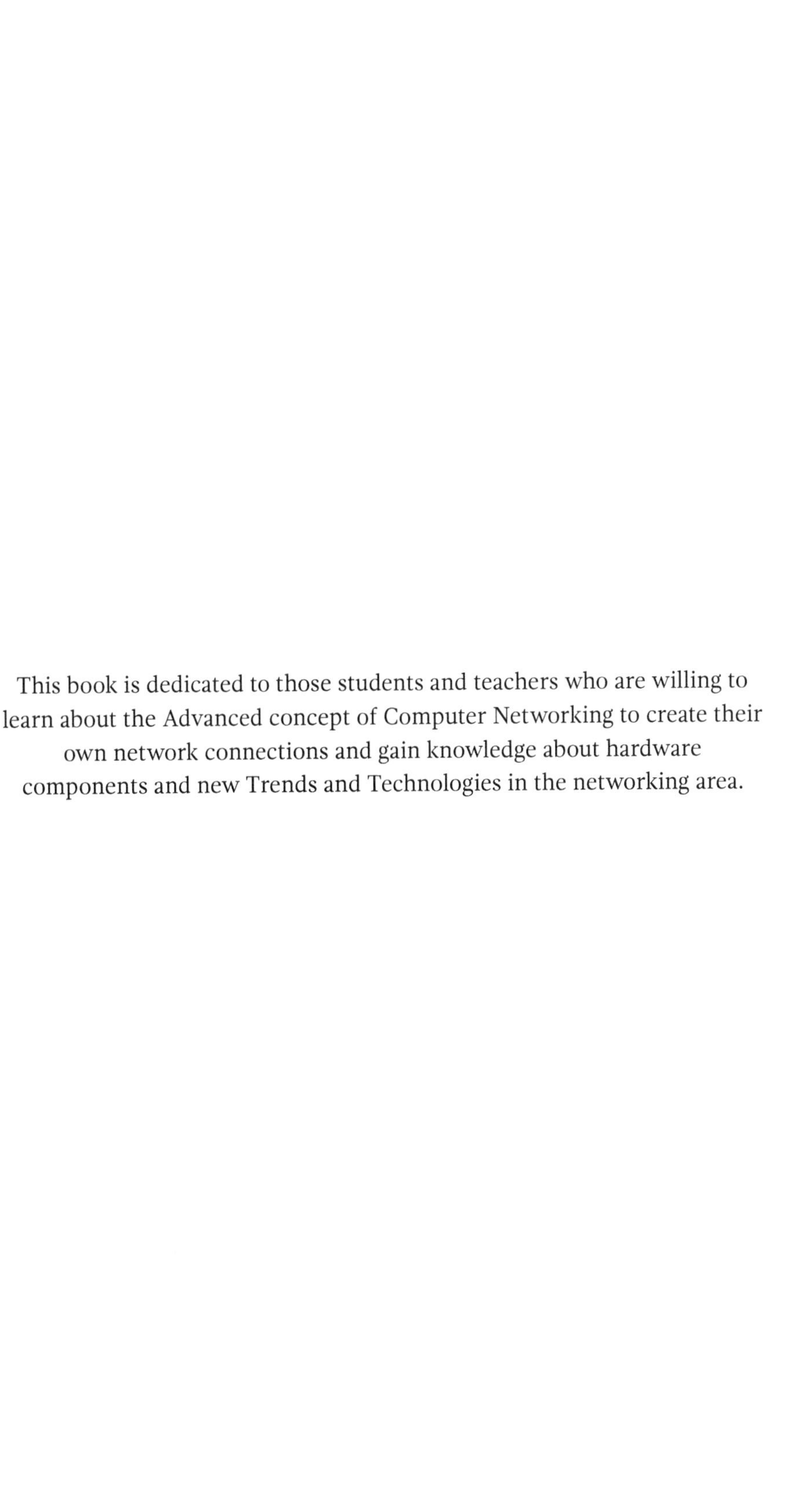

This book is dedicated to those students and teachers who are willing to learn about the Advanced concept of Computer Networking to create their own network connections and gain knowledge about hardware components and new Trends and Technologies in the networking area.

Contents

Foreword

If you want to learn any trend and technologies and you are willing to create any hardware and software application you need to clear your basic with advanced concepts of that particular domain. An advanced Computer network is useful to create connection between many devices and connected applications. You can gain the concepts with different networking strategy with different concepts.

This book fully embraces the potential of the Computer Networks to empower its users. It's a friendly and approachable text intended to help you level up not just your knowledge of basic with Advanced Networking, but also reach your confidence as in networking area. So dive in and get ready to learn and welcome to the Networking community.

Preface

This book is for computer scientists,computer engineers and others who wants to learn about basic with an advanced concepts of Networking area.

Our aim is to explain the enduring concepts underlying all computer system, and to show you the concrete ways that these ideas affect the correctness, performance, and utility of your application programs.This book is written from a devloper's , Networking with cisco packet and wireshark concepts and knowledge perspective.

If you study and learn the concepts in this book, you will be on your way to becoming the rare "power developer" who knows how things work and how to fix them. Our aim is to present the fundamental concepts in ways that you will find useful right away. You will also be prepared to studying such topics as networking models , protocols and its connection based topologies.

Acknowledgements

I would like to express my greatest appreciation to the all individuals who have helped and supported me throughout writing this book. I am thankful to my family members and my colleagues during this book writing for initial advice, and encouragement, which led to the final completion of the book.

I special acknowledgment goes to my motivators Mrs. Hetal Bhaidasna who helped me in completing the book by exchanging interesting ideas and sharing their experience. Also i like to thanks to Parul University from where i got the uncountable and a lot of knowledge.

I would like to thank my special one who always motivated me to do my best in my career also Thank you for always believing in me.

I wish to thank my parents as well for their undivided support and interest who inspired me and encouraged me to go my own way, without whom I would be unable to complete this book.

In the end, I want to thank my friends who displayed appreciation for my work and motivated me to continue my work.

Prologue

In this book the basic details of basic with an Avdnaced Computer Networks is given and it is starting from the basic and an Advanced computer networking and about networking advantages and Disadvantages as well as about architecture and protocols of networking with cisco packets implementations and about IP Address also here decribe about Wireless networks.

Before learning the concepts of networking you aware about some basic Hardware and protocols as well as about some networking connection and security.

It has different versions can exist side by side. It is also Type safe and provides rich libraries of many built in functions.

Using Advanced Computer networks you can create new trending smart systems with security.

CHAPTER ONE

REVIEW OF NETWORKING BASICS

Computer Network: A network comprising various hardware units, usually referred to as hosts, that are connected via various channels in order to send and receive data or media. Network devices, which include things like routers, switches, hubs, and bridges, are another type of device that may be used in computer networks to facilitate communication between two separate machines.

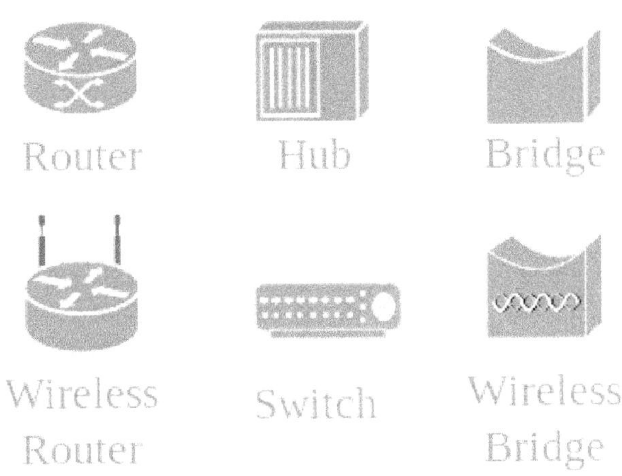

Networking Devices

Open system:
A system that is connected to the network and is ready for communication.

Closed system:

A system that is not connected to the network and can't be communicated with.

Network Topology:

The layout arrangement of the different devices in a network. Common examples include: Bus, Star, Mesh, Ring, and Daisy chain.

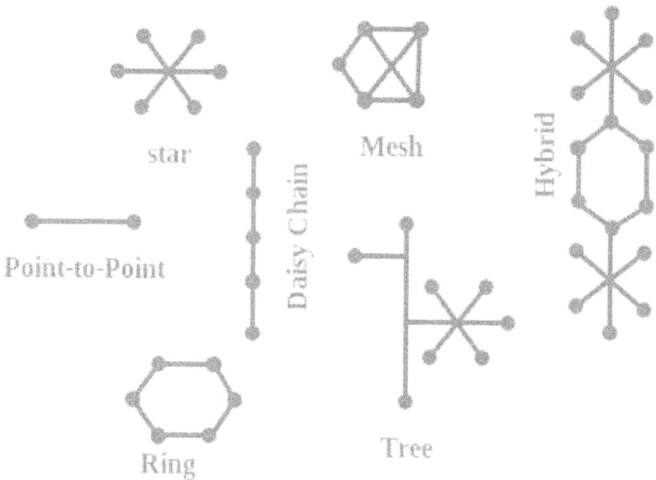

Networks Topology

OSI:

OSI stands for **Open Systems Interconnection**. It is a reference model that specifies standards for communications protocols and also the functionalities of each layer.

Protocol:

A protocol is a set of rules or algorithms which define the way how two entities can communicate across the network and there are different protocols defined at each layer of the OSI model. A few such protocols are TCP, IP, UDP, ARP, DHCP, FTP, and so on.

IP Address (Internet Protocol address):

Also known as the Logical Address, the IP Address is the network address of the system across the network.

To identify each device in the world-wide-web, the Internet Assigned Numbers Authority (IANA) assigns an IPV4 (Version 4) address as a unique identifier to each device on the Internet.

The length of an IPv4 address is 32-bits, hence, we have 2^{32} IP addresses available. The length of an IPv6 address is 128-bits.
Type "ipconfig" in the command prompt and press 'Enter', this gives us the IP address of the device.

MAC Address (Media Access Control address):

Also known as physical address, the MAC Address is the unique identifier of each host and is associated with its NIC (Network Interface Card).
A MAC address is assigned to the NIC at the time of manufacturing.
The length of the MAC address is: 12-nibble/ 6 bytes/ 48 bits
Type "ipconfig/all" in the command prompt and press 'Enter', this gives us the MAC address.

Port:

An application's port may be thought of as a logical channel via which data can be transferred or received. Every programme that is running on a host is identifiable by the port number on which it is active.
A port number is a 16-bit integer, hence, we have 2^{16} ports available which are categorized as shown below:

Port Types	Range
Well known Ports	0 – 1023
Registered Ports	1024 – 49151
Ephemeral Ports	49152 – 65535

Ports with Range

Number of ports: 65,536
Range: 0 – 65535
Type "**netstat -a**" in the command prompt and press 'Enter', this lists all the ports being used.

Socket:

The unique combination of IP address and Port number together is termed as Socket.

DNS Server:

DNS stands for **Domain Name System**.
DNS is basically a server that translates web addresses or URLs (ex: www.google.com) into their corresponding IP addresses. We don't have to

remember all the IP addresses of each and every website.

The command '**nslookup**' gives you the IP address of the domain you are looking for. This also provides information on our DNS Server.

ARP:

ARP stands for **Address Resolution Protocol.**

It is used to convert an IP address to its corresponding physical address (i.e., MAC Address).

ARP is used by the Data Link Layer to identify the MAC address of the Receiver's machine.

RARP:

RARP stands for **Reverse Address Resolution Protocol.**

As the name implies, it outputs the device's IP address when a physical address is supplied. But since DHCP entered the scene, RARP has lost its usefulness.

IPv4:IP stands for **Internet Protocol** and **v4** stands for **Version Four** (IPv4). IPv4 was the primary version brought into action for production within the ARPANET in 1983.

IP version four addresses are 32-bit integers that will be expressed in decimal notation.

Example- 192.0.2.126 could be an IPv4 address.

Parts of IPv4

- **Network part:**

  The network part indicates the distinctive variety that's appointed to the network. The network part conjointly identifies the category of the network that's assigned.
- **Host Part:**

  The host part uniquely identifies the machine on your network. This part of the IPv4 address is assigned to every host.

  For each host on the network, the network part is the same, however, the host half must vary.
- **Subnet number:**

  This is the nonobligatory part of IPv4. Local networks that have massive numbers of hosts are divided into subnets and subnet numbers are appointed to them.

Characteristics of IPv4

- IPv4 could be a 32-Bit IP Address.
- IPv4 could be a numeric address, and its bits are separated by a dot.
- The number of header fields is twelve and the length of the header field is twenty.
- It has Unicast, broadcast, and multicast styles of addresses.
- IPv4 supports VLSM (Virtual Length Subnet Mask).
- IPv4 uses the Post Address Resolution Protocol to map to the MAC address.
- RIP may be a routing protocol supported by the routed daemon.
- Networks ought to be designed either manually or with DHCP.
- Packet fragmentation permits routers and causes host.

Advantages of IPv4

- IPv4 security permits encryption to keep up privacy and security.
- IPV4 network allocation is significant and presently has quite 85000 practical routers.
- It becomes easy to attach multiple devices across an outsized network while not NAT.
- This is a model of communication that provides quality service also as economical knowledge transfer.
- IPV4 addresses are redefined and permit flawless encoding.
- Routing is a lot of scalable and economical as a result of addressing collective more effectively.
- Data communication across the network becomes a lot of specific in multicast organizations
- Limits net growth for existing users and hinders the use of the net for brand-new users.
- Internet Routing is inefficient in IPv4.
- IPv4 has high System Management prices and it's labor-intensive, complex, slow & frequent to errors.
- Security features are nonobligatory.
- Difficulty to feature support for future desires as a result of adding it on is extremely high overhead since it hinders the flexibility to attach everything over IP.

Subnetting and masking: The reverse of subnetting is supernetting. A single large network is partitioned into several smaller subnetworks by subnetting. In Supernetting, multiple networks are combined into a bigger network termed as a Supernetwork or Supernet.

- Subnetting's opposite is called supernetting. Subnetting is the process of breaking up a single large network into several smaller subnetworks. A larger network known as a Supernetwork or Supernet is created by supernetting numerous smaller networks together. More specifically,
- When multiple networks are combined to form a bigger network, it is termed super-netting
- Super netting is used in route aggregation to reduce the size of routing tables and routing table updates
- There are some points which should be kept in mind while supernetting:
- All the Networks should be contiguous.
- The block size of every network should be equal and must be in form of 2^n.
- First Network id should be exactly divisible by whole size of supernet.
- **Example** – Suppose 4 small networks of class C:

  200.1.0.0,

  200.1.1.0,

  200.1.2.0,

  200.1.3.0

  Build a bigger network that has a single Network Id.

  Explanation – Before Supernetting routing table will look like as:

Network Id	Subnet Mask	Interface
200.1.0.0	255.255.255.0	A
200.1.1.0	255.255.255.0	B
200.1.2.0	255.255.255.0	C
200.1.3.0	255.255.255.0	D

First, let's check whether three conditions are satisfied or not:

- **Contiguous:** It is clear that all 256-host networks are continuous with one another. initial network's IP address range is 200.1.0.255 to 200.1.0.0. The next network id is 200.1.1.0 if you add 1 to the final IP address of the previous network, which is 200.1.0.255 + 0.0.0.1. Check to see if the entire network is continuous.

- **Equal size of all network:** As all networks are of class C, so all of them have a size of 256 which is in turn equal to 2^8.
- **First IP address exactly divisible by total size:** When a binary number is divided by 2^n then last n bits are the remainder. Hence in order to prove that first IP address is exactly divisible by while size of Supernet Network. You can check that if last n v=bits are 0 or not.
- In the given example first IP is 200.1.0.0 and whole size of supernet is $4*2^8 = 2^{10}$. If last 10 bits of first IP address are zero then IP will be divisible.
- Last 10 bits of first IP address are zero (highlighted by green color). So 3rd condition is also satisfied.

1. Control and reduce network traffic
2. Helpful to solve the problem of lacking IP addresses
3. Minimizes the routing table

    - It cannot cover a different area of the network when combined
    - All the networks should be in the same class and all IP should be contiguous.

Multicast is a technique of group communication in which the sender simultaneously distributes data to a number of network nodes or recipients. A sort of one-to-many and many-to-many communication called multicasting enables sender or senders to simultaneously deliver data packets to a number of recipients via LANs or WANs. This method aids in reducing the network's data frame.

Multicasting operates similarly to broadcasting, however information is transmitted to targeted or particular network users while multicasting. This operation can be completed by sending separate copies to each user or network node, but doing so is wasteful and might result in an increase in network latency. Multicasting, which allows a single broadcast to be divided up among numerous users to address these drawbacks, therefore limits the signal's capacity.

Applications :

Multicasting is used in many areas like:

1. Internet protocol (IP)
2. Streaming Media

It also supports video conferencing applications and webcasts.

IP Multicast :IP Multicasting is the term used to describe multicasting that occurs online. The internet protocol (IP) is used by these multicast systems to convey data. IP multicasting distributes information across network users via a process called "Multicast trees." A single signal can branch out to the intended receivers via multicast trees. The branches are created at the Internet routers, the branches are created such that the length of the transmission will be minimum.

IP multicasts also use two other essential protocols to function; Internet Group Management Protocol (IGMP), Protocol Independent Multicast (PIM). IGMP allows the recipients to access the data or information. The network routers use PIM to create multicast trees. To sum up, Multicasting is an efficient way of communication; it reduces the bandwidth usage.

IP stands for **Internet Protocol** and **v4** stands for **Version Four** (IPv4). IPv4 was the primary version brought into action for production within the ARPANET in 1983.

IP version four addresses are 32-bit integers that will be expressed in decimal notation.

Example- 192.0.2.126 could be an IPv4 address.

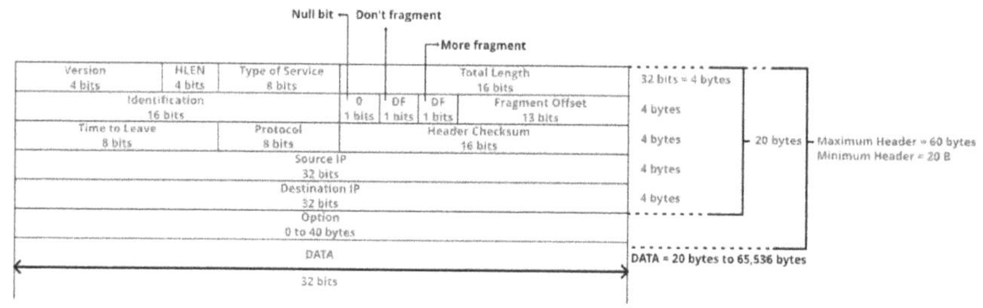

IPV4

Parts of IPv4

- **Network part:**

  The network part indicates the distinctive variety that's appointed to the network. The network part conjointly identifies the category of the network that's assigned.

- **Host Part:**
  The host part uniquely identifies the machine on your network. This part of the IPv4 address is assigned to every host.
  For each host on the network, the network part is the same, however, the host half must vary.
- **Subnet number:**
  This is the nonobligatory part of IPv4. Local networks that have massive numbers of hosts are divided into subnets and subnet numbers are appointed to them.

Characteristics of IPv4

- IPv4 could be a 32-Bit IP Address.
- IPv4 could be a numeric address, and its bits are separated by a dot.
- The number of header fields is twelve and the length of the header field is twenty.
- It has Unicast, broadcast, and multicast styles addresses.
- IPv4 supports VLSM (Virtual Length Subnet Mask).
- IPv4 uses the Post Address Resolution Protocol to map to the MAC address.
- RIP may be a routing protocol supported by the routed daemon.
- Networks ought to be designed either manually or with DHCP.
- Packet fragmentation permits routers and causes host.

Advantages of IPv4

- IPv4 security permits encryption to keep up privacy and security.
- IPV4 network allocation is significant and presently has quite 85000 practical routers.
- It becomes easy to attach multiple devices across an outsized network while not NAT.
- This is a model of communication that provides quality service also as economical knowledge transfer.
- IPV4 addresses are redefined and permit flawless encoding.
- Routing is a lot of scalable and economical as a result of addressing is collective more effectively.
- Data communication across the network becomes a lot of specific in multicast organizations.

- Limits net growth for existing users and hinders the use of the net for brand-new users.
- Internet Routing is inefficient in IPv4.
- IPv4 has high System Management prices and it's labor-intensive, complex, slow & frequent to errors.
- Security features are nonobligatory.
- Difficult to feature support for future desires as a result of adding it on is extremely high overhead since it hinders the flexibility to attach everything over IP.

IP address is an address having information about how to reach a specific host, especially outside the LAN. An IP address is a 32 bit unique address having an address space of 2^{32}.
Generally, there are two notations in which IP address is written, dotted decimal notation and hexadecimal notation.

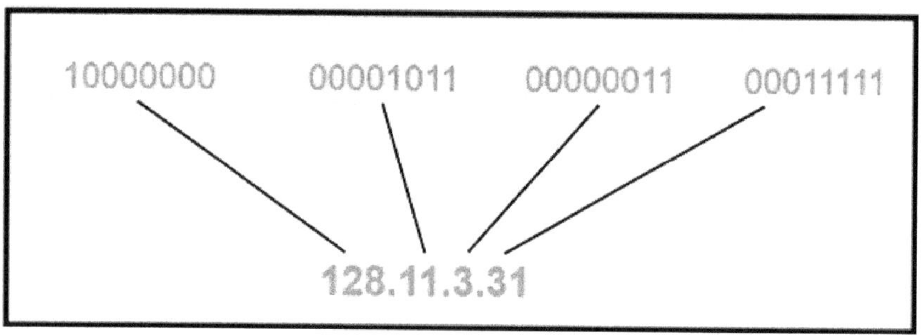

Dotted Decimal Notation

01110101	00011101	10010101	11101010
75	1D	95	EA

0x751D95EA

Hexadecimal Notation

Some points to be noted about dotted decimal notation:

1. The value of any segment (byte) is between 0 and 255 (both included).
2. There are no zeroes preceding the value in any segment (054 is wrong, 54 is correct).

Classful Addressing: The 32 bit IP address is divided into five sub-classes. These are:

- Class A
- Class B
- Class C
- Class D
- Class E

There is a suitable range of IP addresses for each of these classes. For multicast and experimental reasons, respectively, classes D and E are set aside. The classes of IP address are determined by the bit order in the first octet.
The IPv4 address is split into two sections:

- **Network ID**
- **Host ID**

The bits used for network ID and host ID as well as the maximum number of networks and hosts that can be included in a given class of IP address are determined by the class. Each device connected to a network is given an IP address by the ISP or network administrator in charge of that network.

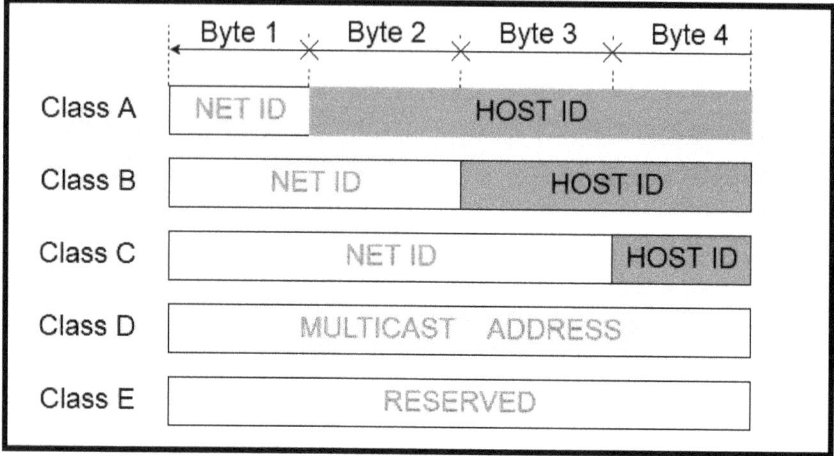

Note: IP addresses are globally managed by Internet Assigned Numbers Authority(IANA) and regional Internet registries(RIR).

Note: Because the first IP address of any network is the network number and the last IP address is designated for broadcast IP, two IP addresses are not considered when determining the total number of host IP addresses and are consequently subtracted from the overall count.

Class A: IP address belonging to class A are assigned to the networks that contain a large number of hosts.

- The network ID is 8 bits long.
- The host ID is 24 bits long.

The higher order bit of the first octet in class A is always set to 0. The remaining 7 bits in first octet are used to determine network ID. The 24 bits of host ID are used to determine the host in any network. The default subnet mask for class A is 255.x.x.x. Therefore, class A has a total of:

- 2^7-2= 126 network ID(Here 2 address is subtracted because 0.0.0.0 and 127.x.y.z are special address.)
- 2^24 – 2 = 16,777,214 host ID

IP addresses belonging to class A ranges from 1.x.x.x – 126.x.x.x

	7 Bit	24 Bit
0	Network	Host

Class A

Class B: IP address belonging to class B are assigned to the networks that ranges from medium-sized to large-sized networks.

- The network ID is 16 bits long.
- The host ID is 16 bits long.

The higher order bits of the first octet of IP addresses of class B are always set to 10. The remaining 14 bits are used to determine network ID. The 16 bits of host ID is used to determine the host in any network. The default sub-net mask for class B is 255.255.x.x. Class B has a total of:

- 2^14 = 16384 network address
- 2^16 – 2 = 65534 host address

IP addresses belonging to class B ranges from 128.0.x.x – 191.255.x.x.

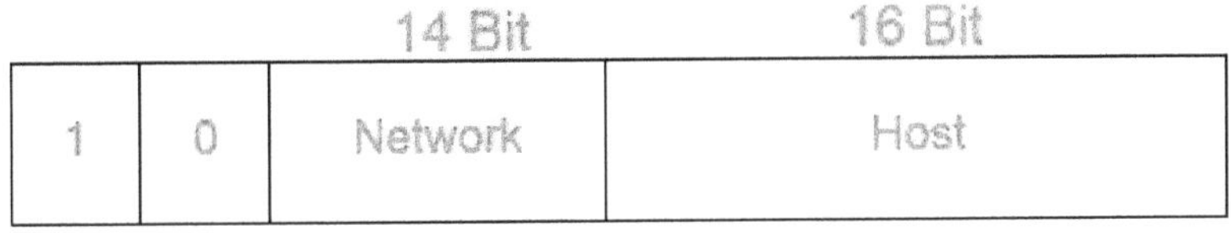

Class B

Class C: IP address belonging to class C are assigned to small-sized networks.

- The network ID is 24 bits long.
- The host ID is 8 bits long.

The higher order bits of the first octet of IP addresses of class C are always set to 110. The remaining 21 bits are used to determine network ID. The 8 bits of host ID is used to determine the host in any network. The default sub-net mask for class C is 255.255.255.x. Class C has a total of:

- 2^21 = 2097152 network address
- 2^8 – 2 = 254 host address

IP addresses belonging to class C ranges from 192.0.0.x – 223.255.255.x.

21 Bit
8 Bit
1
1
0
Network
Host

Class C

Class D: IP address belonging to class D are reserved for multi-casting. The higher order bits of the first octet of IP addresses belonging to class D are always set to 1110. The remaining bits are for the address that interested hosts recognize.

Class D does not posses any sub-net mask. IP addresses belonging to class D ranges from 224.0.0.0 – 239.255.255.255.

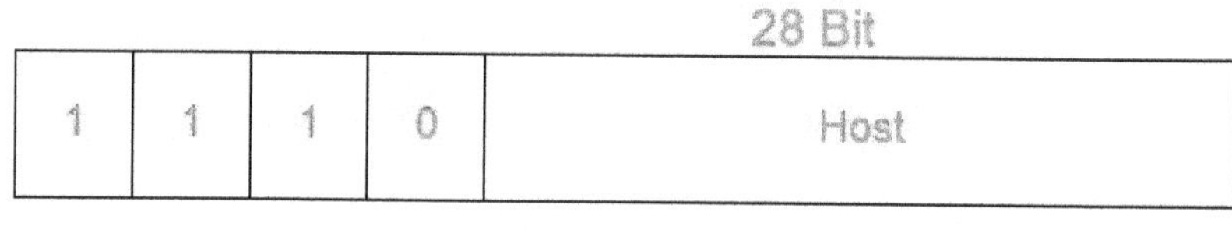

Class D

Class E: IP addresses belonging to class E are reserved for experimental and research purposes. IP addresses of class E ranges from 240.0.0.0 – 255.255.255.254. This class doesn't have any sub-net mask. The higher order bits of first octet of class E are always set to 1111.

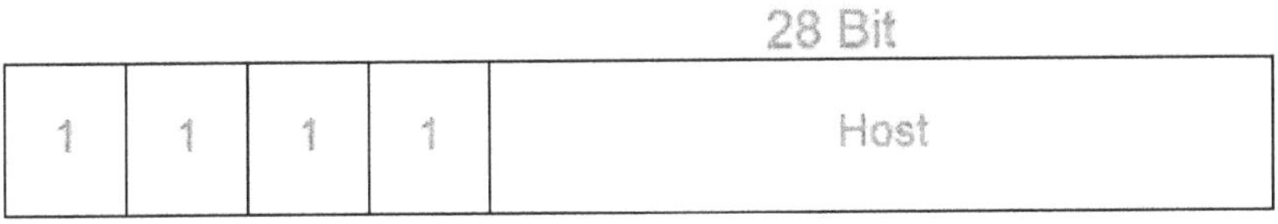

28 Bit

1	1	1	1	Host

Class E

Range of special IP addresses:

169.254.0.0 – 169.254.0.16 : Link local addresses

127.0.0.0 – 127.0.0.8 : Loop-back addresses

0.0.0.0 – 0.0.0.8 : used to communicate within the current network.

Rules for assigning Host ID: Host ID's are used to identify a host within a network. The host ID are assigned based on the following rules:

- Within any network, the host ID must be unique to that network.
- Host ID in which all bits are set to 0 cannot be assigned because this host ID is used to represent the network ID of the IP address.
- Host ID in which all bits are set to 1 cannot be assigned because this host ID is reserved as a broadcast address to send packets to all the hosts present on that particular network.

Rules for assigning Network ID: Hosts that are located on the same physical network are identified by the network ID, as all host on the same physical network is assigned the same network ID. The network ID is assigned based on the following rules:

- The network ID cannot start with 127 because 127 belongs to class A address and is reserved for internal loop-back functions.
- All bits of network ID set to 1 are reserved for use as an IP broadcast address and therefore, cannot be used.
- All bits of network ID set to 0 are used to denote a specific host on the local network and are not routed and therefore, aren't used.

CLASS	LEADING BITS	NET ID BITS	HOST ID BITS	NO. OF NETWORKS	ADDRESSES PER NETWORK	START ADDRESS	END ADDRESS
CLASS A	0	8	24	2^7 (128)	2^{24} (16,777,216)	0.0.0.0	127.255.255.255
CLASS B	10	16	16	2^{14} (16,384)	2^{16} (65,536)	128.0.0.0	191.255.255.255
CLASS C	110	24	8	2^{21} (2,097,152)	2^8 (256)	192.0.0.0	223.255.255.255
CLASS D	1110	NOT DEFINED	NOT DEFINED	NOT DEFINED	NOT DEFINED	224.0.0.0	239.255.255.255
CLASS E	1111	NOT DEFINED	NOT DEFINED	NOT DEFINED	NOT DEFINED	240.0.0.0	255.255.255.255

Summary of Classful addressing

The difficulty with this classful addressing system is that millions of class A addresses are thrown away, along with numerous class B addresses and a dearth of class C addresses that are insufficient to meet the demands of companies. Class D addresses are only accessible in one block since they are utilised for multicast routing. Addresses in the class E are reserved.

Network Address and Mask

Network address – It identifies a network on internet. Using this, we can find range of addresses in the network and total possible number of hosts in the network.

Mask – It is a 32-bit binary number that gives the network address in the address block when AND operation is bitwise applied on the mask and any IP address of the block.

The default mask in different classes are :

Class A – 255.0.0.0

Class B – 255.255.0.0

Class C – 255.255.255.0

Example : Given IP address 132.6.17.85 and default class B mask, find the beginning address (network address).

Solution : The default mask is 255.255.0.0, which means that the only the first 2 bytes are preserved and the other 2 bytes are set to 0. Therefore, the network address is 132.6.0.0.

Subnetting: Subnetting is the process of breaking up a big block of addresses into several contiguous subblocks and allocating these subblocks to various smaller networks. When classless addressing is utilised, this procedure is common.

Classless Addressing: Sub-netting is used to reduce the waste of IP addresses inside a block. We utilise the host id bits of a classful IP address as the net id bits. We give the IP address and define the number of bits for mask along with it (usually followed by a '/' symbol), like, 192.168.1.1/28. Here, subnet mask is found by putting the given number of bits out of 32 as 1, like, in the given address, we need to put 28 out of 32 bits as 1 and the rest as 0, and so, the subnet mask would be 255.255.255.240.

Some values calculated in subnetting :

1. Number of subnets : Given bits for mask – No. of bits in default mask
2. Subnet address : AND result of subnet mask and the given IP address
3. Broadcast address : By putting the host bits as 1 and retaining the network bits as in the IP address
4. Number of hosts per subnet : $2^{(32 - \text{Given bits for mask})} - 2$
5. First Host ID : Subnet address + 1 (adding one to the binary representation of the subnet address)
6. Last Host ID : Subnet address + Number of Hosts

Example : Given IP Address – 172.16.0.0/25, find the number of subnets and the number of hosts per subnet. Also, for the first subnet block, find the subnet address, first host ID, last host ID and broadcast address.

Solution : This is a class B address. So, no. of subnets = $2^{(25-16)} = 2^9 = 512$.

No. of hosts per subnet = $2^{(32-25)} - 2 = 2^7 - 2 = 128 - 2 = 126$

For the first subnet block, we have subnet address = 0.0, first host id = 0.1, last host id = 0.126 and broadcast address = 0.127

Classful Addressing: Introduced in 1981, with classful routing, IP v4 addresses were divided into 5 classes(A to E).

Classes A-C: unicast addresses

Class D: multicast addresses

Class E: reserved for future use

Class A: In a class A address, the first bit of the first octet is always '0'. Thus, class A addresses range from 0.0.0.0 to 127.255.255.255(as 01111111 in binary converts to 127 in decimal). The first 8 bits or the first octet denote the network portion and the rest 24 bits or the 3 octets belong to the host portion. Its Subnet mask is 255.0.0.0.

Example: 10.1.1.1

Exception –

- 127.X.X.X is reserved for loopback
- 0.X.X.X is reserved for the default network

Therefore, the actual range of class A addresses is: 1.0.0.0 to 126.255.255.255

Class B: In a class B address, the first octet would always start with '10'. Thus, class B addresses range from 128.0.0.0 to 191.255.255.255. The first 16 bits or the first two octets denote the network portion and the remaining 16 bits or two octets belong to the host portion. Its Subnet mask is 255.255.0.0.

Example: 172.16.1.1

Class C: In a class C address, the first octet would always start with '110'. Thus, class C addresses range from 192.0.0.0 to 223.255.255.255. The first 24 bits or the first three octets denote the network portion and the rest 8 bits or the remaining one octet belong to the host portion. Its Subnet mask is 255.255.255.0.

Example: 192.168.1.1

Class D: Class D is used for multicast addressing and in class D address the first octet would always start with '1110'. Thus, class D addresses range from 224.0.0.0 to 239.255.255.255. Its Subnet mask is not defined.

Example: 239.2.2.2

Class D addresses are used by routing protocols like OSPF, RIP, etc.

Class E :

Class E addresses are reserved for research purposes and future use. The first octet in a class E address starts with '1111'. Thus, class E addresses range from 240.0.0.0 to 255.255.255.255. Its Subnet mask is not defined.

Disadvantage of Classful Addressing:

1. Class A with a mask of 255.0.0.0 can support 128 Networks, 16,777,216 addresses per network, and a total of 2,147,483,648 addresses.
2. Class B with a mask of 255.255.0.0 can support 16,384 Networks, 65,536 addresses per network, and a total of 1,073,741,824 addresses.
3. Class C with a mask of 255.255.255.0 can support 2,097,152 Networks, 256 addresses per network, and a total of 536,870,912 addresses.

CIDR or Class Inter-Domain Routing was introduced in 1993 to replace classful addressing. It allows the user to use VLSM or Variable Length Subnet Masks.

CIDR notation:

In CIDR subnet masks are denoted by /X. For example a subnet of 255.255.255.0 would be denoted by /24. To work a subnet mask in CIDR, we have to first convert each octet into its respective binary value. For example, if the subnet is of 255.255.255.0. then :

First Octet – 255 has 8 binary 1's when converted to binary

Second Octet – 255 has 8 binary 1's when converted to binary

Third Octet – 255 has 8 binary 1's when converted to binary

Fourth Octet – 0 has 0 binary 1's when converted to binary

Therefore, in total there are 24 binary 1's, so the subnet mask is /24. While creating a network in CIDR, a person has to make sure that the masks are contiguous, i.e. a subnet mask like 10111111.X.X.X can't exist. With CIDR, we can create Variable Length Subnet Masks, leading to less wastage of IP addresses. It is not necessary that the divider between the network and the host portions is at an octet boundary. For example, in CIDR a subnet mask like 255.224.0.0 or 11111111.11100000.00000000.00000000 can exist.

Sr. No.	Parameter	Classful Addressing	Classless Addressing
1.	**Basics**	In Classful addressing IP addresses are allocated according to the classes- A to E.	Classless addressing came to replace the classful addressing and to handle the issue of rapid exhaustion of IP addresses.
2.	**Practical**	It is less practical.	It is more practical.
3.	**Network ID and Host ID**	The changes in the Network ID and Host ID depend on the class.	There is no such restriction of class in classless addressing.
4.	**VLSM**	It does not support the Variable Length Subnet Mask (VLSM).	It supports the Variable Length Subnet Mask (VLSM).
5.	**Bandwidth**	Classful addressing requires more bandwidth. As a result, it becomes slower and more expensive as compared to classless addressing.	It requires less bandwidth. Thus, fast and less expensive as compared to classful addressing.
6.	**CIDR**	It does not support Classless Inter-Domain Routing (CIDR).	It supports Classless Inter-Domain Routing (CIDR).
7.	**Updates**	Regular or periodic updates	Triggered Updates
8.	**Troubleshooting and Problem detection**	Troubleshooting and problem detection are easy than classless addressing because of the division of network, host and subnet parts in the address.	It is not as easy compared to classful addressing.
9.	**Division of Address**	• Network • Host • Subnet	• Host • Subnet

Difference between Classful Addressing and Classless Addressing

IGMP: Internet Group Management Protocol is referred to as IGMP. In order to multicast messages and data packets over IP networks, hosts and nearby routers employ the IGMP communication protocol, which effectively utilises the network's resources. IGMP can be utilised in streaming video, gaming, or web conferencing technologies since multicast communication can have a single or several senders and recipients. This protocol is used on IPv4 networks, whereas Multicast Listener Discovery controls multicasting on IPv6 networks (MLD). IGMP is utilised on the network layer, just as other network protocols. MLDv1 and MLDv2 work substantially identically to IGMPv2 and IGMPv3, respectively.The communication protocol, IGMPv1 was developed in 1989 at Stanford University. IGMPv1 was updated to IGMPv2 in year 1997 and again updated to IGMPv3 in year 2002.

Applications:

- **Streaming** – Multicast routing protocol are used for audio and video streaming over the network i.e., either one-to-many or many-to-many.
- **Gaming** – Internet group management protocol is often used in simulation games which has multiple users over the network such as online games.
- **Web Conferencing tools** – Video conferencing is a new method to meet people from your own convenience and IGMP connects to the users for conferencing and transfers the message/data packets efficiently.

Types: There are 3 versions of IGMP. These versions are backward compatible. Following are the versions of IGMP:

1. IGMPv1 : The IGMP communication protocol version includes several fundamental capabilities and enables all supported sites to join multicast groups using membership requests. However, the host is unable to quit the group on their own and must wait for a timeout before doing so. The message packet format in IGMPv1:

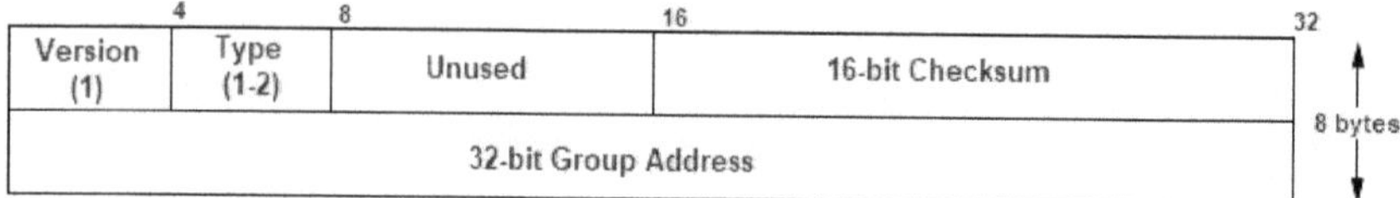

- **Version** – Set to 1.
- **Type** – 1 for Host Membership Query and Host Membership Report.
- **Unused** – 8-bits of zero which are of no use.
- **Checksum** – It is the one's complement of the sum of IGMP messages.
- **Group Address** – The group address field is zero when sent and ignored when received in the membership query message. In a membership report message, the group address field takes the IP host group address of the group being reported.

2. IGMPv2 : IGMPv2 is the revised version of IGMPv1 communication protocol. It has added functionality of leaving the multicast group using group membership. The message packet format in IGMPv2:

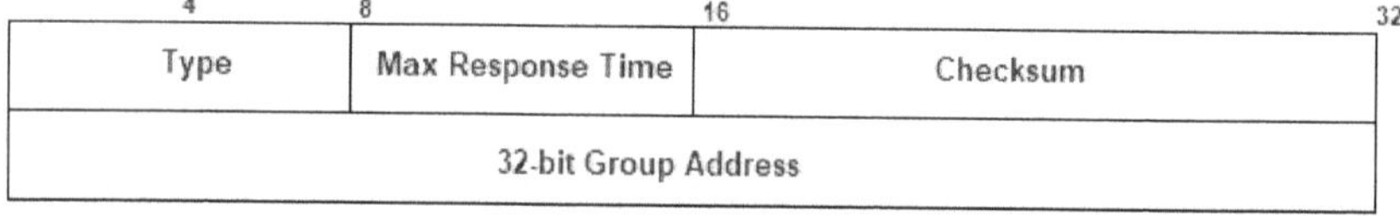

Type:
0x11 for Membership Query
0x12 for IGMPv1 Membership Report
0x16 for IGMPv2 Membership Report
0x22 for IGMPv3 Membership Report

0x17 for Leave Group

- **Max Response Time** – This field is ignored for message types other than membership query. For membership query type, it is the maximum time allowed before sending a response report. The value is in units of 0.1 seconds.
- **Checksum** – It is the one's complement of the sum of IGMP message.
- **Group Address** – It is set as 0 when sending a general query. Otherwise, multicast address for group-specific or source-specific queries.

3. IGMPv3 : IGMPv2 was revised to IGMPv3 and added source-specific multicast and membership report aggregation. These reports are sent to 224.0.0.22. The message packet format in IGMPv3:

IGMPv3 Packet Format

Bit Offset	0-3	4	5-7	8-15	16-31
0	Type = 0x11			Max Response Code	Checksum
32	Group Address				
64	Resv	S	QRV	QQIC	Number of Sources (N)
96	Source Address[1]				
128	Source Address[2]				
	Source Address[N]				

- **Max Response Time** – This field is ignored for message types other than membership query. For membership query type, it is the maximum time allowed before sending a response report. The value is in units of 0.1 seconds.
- **Checksum** – It is the one's complement of the one's complement of the sum of IGMP message.
- **Group Address** – It is set as 0 when sending a general query. Otherwise, multicast address for group-specific or source-specific queries.

- **Resv** – It is set zero of sent and ignored when received.
- **S flag** – It represents Suppress Router-side Processing flag. When the flag is set, it indicates to suppress the timer updates that multicast routers perform upon receiving any query.
- **QRV** – It represents Querier's Robustness Variable. Routers keeps on retrieving the QRV value from the most recently received query as their own value until the most recently received QRV is zero.
- **QQIC** – It represents Querier's Query Interval Code.
- **Number of sources** – It represents the number of source addresses present in the query. For general query or group-specific query, this field is zero and for group-and-source-specific query, this field is non-zero.
- **Source Address[i]** – It represents the IP unicast address for N fields.

Working: IGMP operates on hardware that can handle dynamic multicasting and multicast groups. These gadgets enable the host to join or depart the multicast group membership. Additionally, these tools enable adding and removing clients from the group. The local multicast router and the host implement this communication mechanism. When a multicast group is formed, its address, which is relayed as the packet's destination IP address and falls inside the class D (224-239) IP address range, is generated.

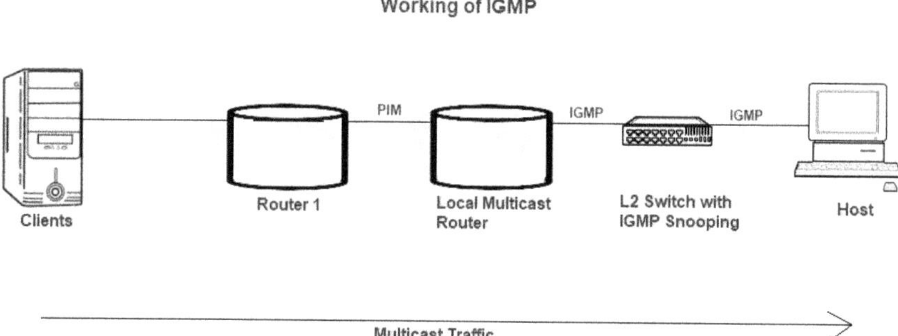

L2 or Level-2 devices such as switches are used in between host and multicast router for IGMP snooping. IGMP snooping is a process to listen to the IGMP network traffic in controlled manner. Switch receives the message from host and forwards the membership report to the local multicast router. The multicast traffic is further forwarded to remote routers from local multicast routers using PIM (Protocol Independent Multicast) so that clients can receive the message/data packets. Clients wishing to join the network sends join message in the query and switch intercepts the message and adds the ports of clients to its multicast routing table.

Advantages:

- IGMP communication protocol efficiently transmits the multicast data to the receivers and so, no junk packets are transmitted to the host which shows optimized performance.
- Bandwidth is consumed totally as all the shared links are connected.
- Hosts can leave a multicast group and join another.

Disadvantages:

- It does not provide good efficiency in filtering and security.
- Due to lack of TCP, network congestion can occur.
- IGMP is vulnerable to some attacks such as DOS attack (Denial-Of-Service).

PIM: Protocol Independent Multicast (PIM) is a collection of multicast routing protocols, each optimized for a different environment. There are two main PIM protocols, PIM Sparse Mode and PIM Dense Mode. A third PIM protocol, Bi-directional PIM, is less widely used.

Typically, either PIM Sparse Mode or PIM Dense Mode will be used throughout a multicast domain. However, they may also be used together within a single domain, using Sparse Mode for some groups and Dense Mode for others. This mixed-mode configuration is known as Sparse-Dense Mode. Similarly, Bi-directional PIM may be used on its own, or it may be used in conjunction with one or both of PIM Sparse Mode and PIM Dense Mode.

All PIM protocols share a common control message format. PIM control messages are sent as raw IP datagrams (protocol number 103), either multicast to the link-local ALL PIM ROUTERS multicast group, or unicast to a specific destination.

PIM Sparse Mode (PIM-SM) is a multicast routing technology that is built on the premise that recipients for any given multicast group would be sporadically dispersed over the network. Therefore, it is believed that the majority of network subnets would reject any given multicast packet.

Routers must actively inform their upstream peers of their interest in certain groups and sources in order to receive multicast data. PIM Join and Prune messages are used by routers to join and prune multicast distribution trees.

All sources sending to the multicast group utilise shared trees by default, which are multicast distribution trees anchored at a particular node (in PIM, this router is known as the Rendezvous Point, or RP). Sources must package data in PIM control messages and deliver it by unicast to the RP in order to send it to the RP. The source's Designated Router (DR), a router on the source's local network, performs this. A single DR is elected from all PIM routers on a network, so that unnecessary control messages are not sent. One of the important requirements of PIM Sparse Mode, and Bi-directional PIM, is the ability to discover the address of a RP for a multicast group using a shared tree. Various RP discovery mechanisms are used, including static configuration, Bootstrap Router, Auto-RP, Anycast RP, and Embedded RP.

PIM-SM also supports the use of source-based trees, in which a separate multicast distribution tree is built for each source sending data to a multicast group. Each tree is rooted at a router adjacent to the source, and sources send data directly to the root of the tree. Source-based trees enable the use of Source-Specific Multicast (SSM), which allows hosts to specify the source from which they wish to receive data, as well as the multicast group they wish to join. With SSM, a host identifies a multicast data stream with a source and group address pair (S,G), rather than by group address alone (*,G).

PIM-SM may use source-based trees in the following circumstances.

- For SSM, a last-hop router will join a source-based tree from the outset.
- To avoid data sent to an RP having to be encapsulated, the RP may join a source-based tree.
- To optimize the data path, a last-hop router may choose to switch from the shared tree to a source-based tree.

A soft-state protocol is PIM-SM. In other words, after receiving the control message that established it, all state is timed-out. All PIM Join messages are regularly retransmitted in order to maintain the status. Version 1 of PIM-SM was created in 1995, but was never standardized by the IETF. It is now considered obsolete, though it is still supported by Cisco and Juniper routers. Version 2 of PIM-SM was standardized in RFC 2117 (in 1997) and updated by RFC 2362 (in 1998). Version 2 is significantly different from and incompatible with version 1. However, there were a number of problems with RFC 2362, and a new specification of PIM-SM version 2 is currently being produced by the IETF. There have been many implementations of PIM-SM and it is widely used.

DVMRP: The distance vector multicast routing protocol is multicast routing protocol that takes the routing decision based upon the source address of the packet.

• This algorithm constructs the routing tree for a network.

• Whenever a router receives a packet, it forwards it to some of its ports based on the source address of packet.

The rest of the routing tree is made by downstream routers.

• In this way, routing tree is created from destination to source.

• The protocol must achieve the following tasks:

1. It must prevent the formation of loops in the network.
2. It must prevent the formation of duplicate packets.
3. It must ensure that the path traveled by a packet is the shortest from its source to the router.
4. It should provide dynamic membership.

To accomplish this, the DVMR algorithm uses a process based on following decision making strategies:

1. Reverse Path Forwarding (RPF)

• In this strategy, the router only forwards those packets that have traveled the shortest path from source to destination.

• To achieve this, the router pretends that it has a packet to send to the source from where the packet has arrived.

• In this way, the shortest path to the sender of the packet is computed.

• If the same route is followed by the received packet, it is forwarded to the next router and it is discarded otherwise.

• The reverse path forwarding ensures that the network receives a copy of the packet without formation of loops. A loop occurs when a packet that has left the router may come back again from another interface or the same interface and be forwarded again.

• RPF does not guarantee that there would be no duplicate packets in the network i.e. the network may receive two or more copies.

• The reason for this is that the routing is based on the source address and not on the destination address.

2. Reverse Path Broadcasting (RPB)

• In order to solve the problem, RPB is used.

• In this method, one parent router is defined for each network.

• The network could accept the multicast packets from this parent router only.

• This router sends packets to those ports for which it is designated as a parent. Thus, RPB principle' allows a router to broadcast the packet in the network.

This creates duplicate packets on the network and reduces network efficiency.

3. Reverse Path Multicasting (RPM)

• To overcome the problem of broadcasting in RPB, Reverse Path Multicasting in used.

• In this the desired multicast network tree is created by using two different methods: Pruning and grafting.

• A router can send a prune message to its upstream router whenever it finds that its network is not interested in a multicast packet. In this way a router prunes (cuts) its network from multicasting.

• If a router receives a prune message from all the downstream routers, it in turn, sends a prune message to its upstream router.

• A router can also send a graft message to its upstream router if it finds that its network is again interested in receiving the multicast packet. In this way, the graft message forces the upstream router to resume sending the multicast message. The network is again grafted (joined).

4. Multicast Open Shortest Path First (MOSPF)

• Multicast open shortest path first is the multicast version of open shortest path first protocol.

• It is an extension of OSPF that uses a multicast link-state routing method to create source-based trees.

• The method used by MOSPF is different from DVMRP.

• The first difference is· that in this method, the tree is the least cost tree instead of the shortest path tree.

• The second .difference is that the tree is not made gradually. It is made immediately it is prepruned and ready to use.

CHAPTER TWO

TELECOM NETWORKS

Telecom networks: Today, wide-area communications are mostly carried out by telecom networks. It was not a wise long-term plan to string a cable between every possible pair of telephones that wanted to communicate. Connecting every phone to a central switching centre was a superior concept. There, a switchboard allowed an operator to connect one phone to another.

Routing a telephone call: A call is routed up via higher-level switching offices until it reaches a switching office that can link with lower-level switching offices to reach the destination telephone. These switching offices make these judgments by looking at the digits of the phone number you dialled.

Connection-Oriented Services – I : The endpoints remain connected exclusively during the session. This often indicates that the bandwidth for the established channel can fairly ensure the quality of service. Bits of the message are received in the same sequence as they were sent. A conventional phone circuit is a connection-oriented, circuit-switched system.

Transmission Media in Telephone Systems: Category 3 UTP cables are used to link the telephone to the local exchange in conventional analogue telephone networks. The local loop is the name of this link. It usually ranges in length from 1 to 10 kilometres. To carry several phone calls further up the hierarchy, greater bandwidth connections are utilised. Compared to having separate wires for each call, this is far less expensive. Particularly, fiber-based digital lines are employed. This was accomplished by analogue systems using a method known as frequency division multiplexing (FDM).

The local loop: The battery bank in the exchange powers the subscriber handsets. Half-duplex transmission is used with echo suppressors. Full-duplex communication is achievable using echo cancellers. For transferring digital data, we require modems because the local loop is still analogue. Since one bit is utilised for control, the typical speed is 56 kbps. Modems could automatically negotiate a slower speed depending on the state of the line.

Signaling: Signaling describes the information exchanges that take place between terminal devices, exchanges, and routers to set up circuits, terminate connections, charge for services, among other things. Some of the frame's bits are used for this in band-wide common channel signalling, of which SS7 is regarded as standard. The switch controllers might theoretically be viewed as an overlay network on the control plane, whether they operate in-band or out-of-band. Out of band signalling, also known as CCIS (Common Channel Interoffice Signaling), is more adaptable since it enables the transport of arbitrary complex messages without interfering with the conventional channel.

Control Plane Protocol Stack in SS7:

- **Application Service Element (ASE)** – Application-level functionality such as interpreting signaling messages. Transaction Capabilities Application Part(TCAP) allows the system to invoke procedure calls on remote machines.
- **Message Transfer Part 1 (MTP-1)** – it is a physical bit transfer usually on a digital line like E1. One of the main applications of SS7 is Telephone User Part (TUP) which is responsible for setting up voice calls. The TUP interprets dialed digits, routes, reserves resources, maintains accounts, etc.

Digital Technology in Telephone Networks: The conventional analogue telephone network has been mostly supplanted by digital technology during the past 30 years. To transform analogue voice signals into digital information that can be processed by digital technology, a device known as a codec (coder/decoder) is employed. The codec is also used to convert the digital signals back into analog voice signals that can be handled by the older analog technology.

In the past 30 years, digital technology has mostly replaced the traditional analogue telephone network. Using a device known as a codec (coder/decoder), analogue voice signals are converted into digital data that can be handled by digital technology. The codec is also used to transform digital communications back into analogue voice signals so that the more antiquated analogue equipment can handle them.

Digital Subscriber Loop:

The next attempt for converting the analog local loop went in two directions:

1. Large users could be serviced by taking fiber to their premises which could terminate on an integrated digital outlet.
2. The market for small users was driven by the demand for more bandwidth from the subscriber for Internet connection over the same Cat3 cable.

Switching Techniques: Switched communication networks convey data from a source to a destination through a number of intermediary nodes. The method through which nodes control or switch data to send it between particular places on a network is known as switching. There are 3 common switching techniques:

1. Circuit Switching
2. Packet Switching
3. Message Switching

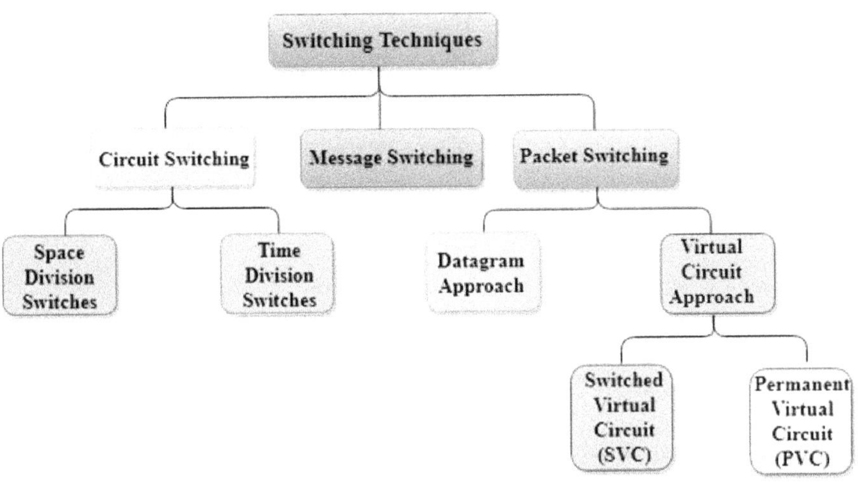

Message Switching –Before packet switching was invented, a technology called message switching was created as an alternative to circuit switching. When using message switching, end users converse by sending and receiving messages that contain all of the shared data. The smallest individual unit is a message. Additionally, there is no direct connection between the sender and receiver. Many intermediary nodes transfer data and make sure the message gets to its intended location. Message switched data networks are hence called hop-by-hop systems.

They provide 2 distinct and important characteristics:

1. **Store and forward** – The task of sending the complete message to the following node falls on the intermediate nodes. As a result, each node has to have storage space. If the following hop and the connection that connects them are unavailable, a message won't be sent and will instead be kept indefinitely. Only when adequate resources are available and the following hop is accepting data does a store-and-forward switch forward a message. The store-and-forward property is what is meant by this.
2. **Message delivery** – This entails sending a single message including all the data from the source to the destination nodes. The source and destination of each message must be included in the header, which also carries the message routing information. Message switching network consists of transmission links (channels), store-and-forward switch nodes, and end stations as shown in the following picture:

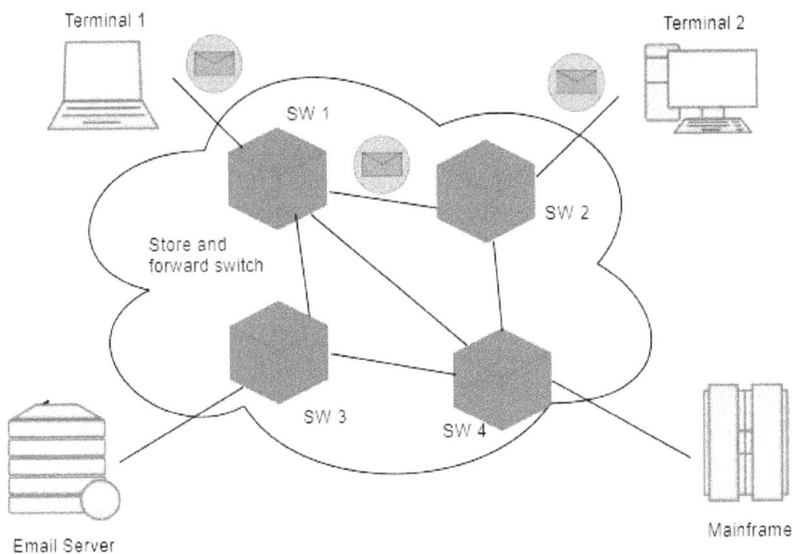

Characteristics of message switching –Message switching has benefits because it makes it possible to use network resources effectively. Additionally, the capacity of intermediary nodes to store and send data allows for effective regulation and management of traffic. Another advantage is that messages are sent as a whole rather than in bits. Message switching, however, also has certain drawbacks. Switches need a lot of storage space since messages are permanently saved at each intermediary node. These are also rather sluggish. This is because at each node, first there is a wait till the entire message is received, then it must be stored and transmitted after processing the next node and links to it depending on availability and channel traffic. Hence, message switching cannot be used for real-time or interactive applications like a video conference.

Advantages of Message Switching –

Message switching has the following advantages:

1. As message switching is able to store the message for which communication channel is not available, it helps in reducing the traffic congestion in the network.
2. In message switching, the data channels are shared by the network devices.

3. It makes traffic management efficient by assigning priorities to the messages.
4. Because the messages are delivered via a store and forward method, it is possible to include priority in them.
5. It allows for infinite message lengths.
6. Unlike circuit switching, it does not necessitate the actual connection of source and destination devices.

Disadvantages of Message Switching –

Message switching has the following disadvantages:

1. Message switching cannot be used for real-time applications as storing messages causes delay.
2. In message switching, the message has to be stored for which every intermediate device in the network requires a large storing capacity.
3. Because the system is so intricate, people are frequently unaware of whether or not messages are correctly conveyed. This could cause problems in social relationships.
4. The type of message switching does not create a dedicated path between the devices. It is not dependable communication because there is no direct relationship between sender and receiver.

Applications –

In telegraph message-switching centers, the store-and-forward technique was used. Today's main networks and systems can include message-switching-based delivery mechanisms even if many of them are packet- or circuit-switched networks. For example, in most electronic mail systems the delivery process is based on message switching, while the network is in fact either circuit-switched or packet-switched.

Frame Relay: A packet-switching network technology called Frame Relay is intended to operate at the network's data link layer. It is utilized to carry data through Wide Area Networks and link Local Area Networks (LANs) (WANs). When linking many nodes that need unique dedicated links to be built between each pair of nodes, it is a better option than a point-to-point network. Different-sized packets of data can be sent, and bandwidth can be allocated dynamically. Additionally, it offers a congestion control system to lessen network overheads brought on by congestion. It lacks an error-control and flow-management system.

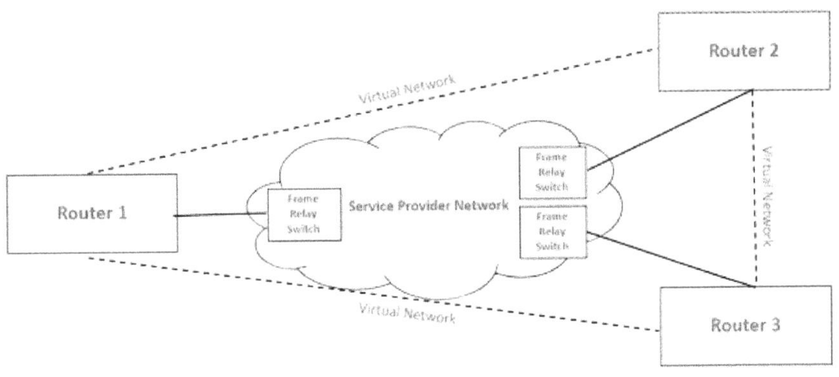

Frame Relay Network

Working:

Frame relay switches provide virtual circuits to link several LANs together to create a WAN. Frame relay divides the data into packets known as frames and transmits these packets over the network to transport data between LANs across WAN. It supports communication with multiple LANs over the shared physical links or private lines.

Between Local Area Networks (LANs) border devices, such as routers, and the service provider network, which links all of the LAN networks, a frame relay network is built. Each LAN has an access link that links its routers to the frame relay switch-terminated service provider network. The private physical link known as the access link is employed for LAN network to LAN network communication across WAN. The access link must be terminated, and frame relay services must be offered, by the frame relay switch.

The LAN router (or any border device connected to the access connection) transmits data by sending packets across the access link. A frame relay switch examines the packet transmitted via LAN to determine its destination using the Data Link Connection Identifier (DLCI). Frame relay switch determines the destination LAN by examining the DLCI of the data packet since it already knows the addresses of the LANs connected to the network. In essence, DLCI detects the virtual circuit between the source and destination networks (i.e., the logical path connecting nodes that don't really exist). It configures and transmits the packet to frame relay switch of destination LAN which in turn transfers the data packet to destination

LAN by sending it over its respective access link. Hence, in this way, a LAN is connected with multiple other LANs by sharing a single physical link for data transmission.

Frame relay also deals with congestion within a network. Following methods are used to identify congestion within a network:

1. **Forward Explicit Congestion Network (FECN)** –The FECN field in the frame header is used to inform the destination of network congestion. The frame relay switch of the destination network sets the FECN bit of the packet whenever a frame encounters congestion during transmission, enabling the destination to recognise that the packet encountered some congestion during transmission.
2. **Backward Explicit Congestion Network (BECN)** –The BECN field in the frame header is used to inform the source of network congestion. When a frame is congested during transmission, the destination sends a frame back to the source with the BECN bit set, letting the source know that the frame was congested while being transferred to the destination. When the source detects congestion in the virtual circuit, the transmission is slowed to prevent network overhead.
3. **Discard Eligibility (DE)** –The frame header's DE field is used to specify the order in which packets should be discarded. The source can set the DE bits of less important packets to signal a high priority for discarding the packets in the event of network overhead if it is producing a lot of traffic on a particular virtual network. In the event of network congestion, packets with set DE bits are dropped before those with unset DE bits.

Types:

1. **Permanent Virtual Circuit (PVC)** –These are the long-lasting, permanent links between frame relay nodes. Even when not in use, they are always open for conversation. These connections are static and do not change with time.
2. **Switched Virtual Circuit (SVC)** –These are the short-term connections between frame relay nodes that are opened only when nodes are in contact with one another and are closed or discarded after the communication has ended. According to the needs, these links are dynamically formed.

Advantages:

1. High speed
2. Scalable
3. Reduced network congestion
4. Cost-efficient
5. Secured connection

Disadvantages:

1. Lacks error control mechanism
2. Delay in packet transfer
3. Less reliable

Why ATM networks?

1. Driven by the integration of services and performance requirements of both telephony and data networking: "broadband integrated service vision" (B-ISON).
2. Telephone networks support a single quality of service and are expensive to boot.
3. Internet supports no quality of service but is flexible and cheap.
4. ATM networks were meant to support a range of service qualities at a reasonable cost- intended to subsume both the telephone network and the Internet.

Asynchronous Transfer Mode (ATM):

It is a call relay system developed by the International Telecommunication Union-Telecommunications Standards Section (ITU-T) that sends all data, including different service kinds like data, video, or voice, in the form of cells, which are tiny fixed-size packets. The network is connection-oriented and cells are sent in an asynchronous manner.

ATM is a technology that has some event in the development of broadband ISDN in the 1970s and 1980s, which can be considered an evolution of packet switching. Each cell is 53 bytes long, with a header of 5 bytes and a payload of 48 bytes. Making an ATM call requires first sending a message to set up a connection.

Each cell then travels the same route to its destination. It can manage both traffic with constant rates and traffic with changing rates. Thus it can carry multiple types of traffic with end-to-end quality of service. ATM is independent of a transmission medium, they may be sent on a wire or fiber by themselves or they may also be packaged inside the payload of other carrier systems. ATM networks use "Packet" or "cell" Switching with virtual circuits. Its design helps in the implementation of high-performance multimedia networking.

ATM Cell Format –

As information is transmitted in ATM in the form of fixed-size units called **cells**. As known already each cell is 53 bytes long which consists of a 5 bytes header and 48 bytes payload.

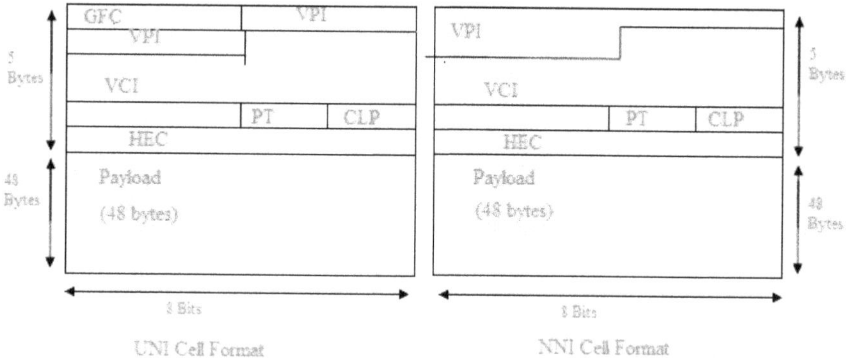

1. **UNI Header:** This is used within private networks of ATMs for communication between ATM endpoints and ATM switches. It includes the Generic Flow Control (GFC) field.
2. **NNI Header:** is used for communication between ATM switches, and it does not include the Generic Flow Control(GFC) instead it includes a Virtual Path Identifier (VPI) which occupies the first 12 bits.

Working of ATM:

There are two types of connections in the ATM standard. i.e., virtual path connections (VPCs), which are essentially bundles of virtual channel connections (VCCs) that transmit a single stream of cells from one user to another. Due to the fact that an ATM network does not route the cells to a specific virtual circuit, a virtual path can be constructed end-to-end throughout the network. All cells associated with a certain virtual channel are sent through the ATM network in the same direction in the event of a significant breakdown, facilitating quicker recovery.

In order to create a virtual trunk between the switches so that they can be managed as a single unit, switches linked to subscribers employ both VPIs and VCIs to switch the cells, which are Virtual Path and Virtual Connection switches that can have various virtual channel connections between them. Its fundamental operation is simple and involves finding the connection value in the local translation table, which reveals the connection's outgoing port and new VPI/VCI value for that link.

ATM vs DATA Networks (Internet) –

- ATM is a "virtual circuit" based: the path is reserved before transmission. While Internet Protocol (IP) is connectionless and end-to-end resource reservations are not possible. RSVP is a new signaling protocol on the internet.
- ATM Cells: Fixed or small size and Tradeoff is between voice or data. While IP packets are of variable size.

Addressing: ATM uses 20-byte global NSAP addresses for signaling and 32-bit locally assigned labels in cells. While IP uses 32-bit global addresses in all packets.

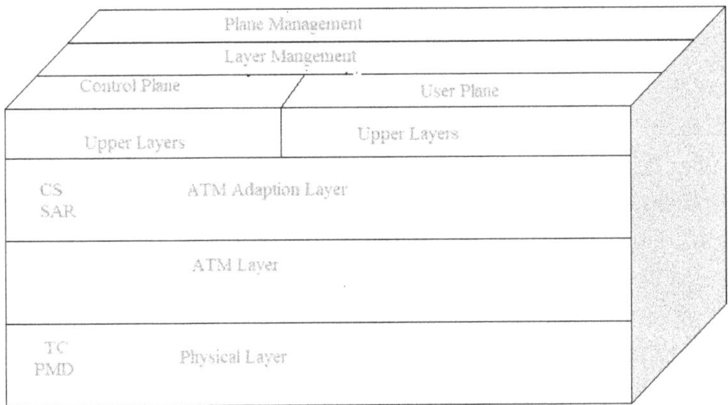

ATM Layers

1. **ATM Adaption Layer (AAL) –**
   It is meant for isolating higher-layer protocols from details of ATM processes and prepares for conversion of user data into cells and segments it into 48-byte cell payloads. AAL protocol excepts transmission from upper-layer services and helps them in mapping applications, e.g., voice, data to ATM cells.
2. **Physical Layer –**
   It manages the medium-dependent transmission and is divided into two parts physical medium-dependent sublayer and transmission convergence sublayer. The main functions are as follows:

   - It converts cells into a bitstream.
   - It controls the transmission and receipt of bits in the physical medium.
   - It can track the ATM cell boundaries.
   - Look for the packaging of cells into the appropriate type of frames.

3. **ATM Layer** – It is responsible for simultaneous virtual circuit sharing over the physical link known as cell multiplexing and passing cells through an ATM network known as cell relay using the VPI and VCI information in the cell header. It also handles transmission, switching, congestion control, cell header processing, sequential delivery, etc.

ATM Applications:

1. **ATM WANs –**
   It can be used as a WAN to send cells over long distances, a router serving as an end-point between ATM network and other networks, which has two stacks of the protocol.
2. **Multimedia virtual private networks and managed services –**
   It helps in managing ATM, LAN, voice, and video services and is capable of full-service virtual private networking, which includes integrated access to multimedia.
3. **Frame relay backbone –**
   Frame relay services are used as a networking infrastructure for a range of data services and enabling frame-relay ATM service to

Internetworking services.

4. **Residential broadband networks –**
   ATM is by choice provides the networking infrastructure for the establishment of residential broadband services in the search of highly scalable solutions.
5. **Carrier infrastructure for telephone and private line networks –**
   To make more effective use of SONET/SDH fiber infrastructures by building the ATM infrastructure for carrying the telephonic and private-line traffic.

MLPS: The IP packet routing method known as Multi Protocol Label Switching (MPLS) uses labels to direct IP packets along paths rather than relying on routers‘ intricate routing tables. This function aids in speeding up IP packet delivery. MPLS employs a router as a forwarding device and a layer 3 service, or Internet Protocol. Due of MPLS's resemblance to a VPN, distinct clients' traffic is kept isolated from one another. Instead of encrypting the data like a typical VPN does, it makes sure that no packet sent by one client may be received by another. Between layers 2 and 3, a packet gains an MPLS header. Hence, it is also considers to be Layer 2.5 protocol.

MPLS Header: The MPLS Header is 32 bit long and is divided into four parts –

1. **Label –** This field is 20 bit long and can take value b/w 0 & $2^{20} - 1$.
2. **Exp –** They are 3 bits long and used for Quality of Service(QoS).
3. **Bottom of stack (S) –** It is of size 1 bit. MPLS labels are stacked one over other. If there is only one label remained in MPLS header, then its value is 1 otherwise 0.
4. **Time to Live (TTL) –** It is 8 bit long and its value is decreased by one at each hop to prevent packet to get stuck in network.

Important terms used in MPLS :

- Provider Edge(PE) Router: Router at edge of MPLS network that add or remove label from IP packet.
- Customer Edge(CE) Router : Router at edge of customer network that send or receive IP packet from PE.

- Label Switch Router(LSR): Routers used in MPLS network that can understand labels.
- Ingress LSR: LSR routers that receive IP packet from CE Routers and add MPLS header.
- Intermediate LSR: LSR routers that swap label in MPLS header and assigned for forwarding labeled IP packet.
- Egress LSR: LSR routers that send IP packet to CE routers and removes MPLS header.
- Push, Pop and Swap: Action of addition, removal and swapping of labels by LSR respectively.

Multiprotocol Label Switching (MPLS) Routing:

Forwarding in MPLS : The link-layer, or layer 2 frames, are encapsulated by LSRs once they receive IP packet CE and add an MPLS header between layer 3 and layer 2. This capability, known as multi-protocol, enables LSRs to support receiving packets including frames from many protocols, including Frame Relay, Metro Ethernet, etc.

Labels connected to IP packets are the foundation of MPLS forwarding. Label Distribution Protocol, a protocol, governs this label attachment (LDP). Each LSR initially learns routes as normal routers do. This learning starts with PE routers. Each PE router learns routes to different subnets from CE router. Suppose PE router PE1 learns route to subnet (say subnet1) from CE router. Now PE1 will add label to packet, forward to its neighboring LSR, and tells them that if you receive packet which destination address to subnet1 then forward it to me.

This LSR repeats the operation once again. LSR acquires routes in this manner and adds this data to the Label Forwarding Information Base (LFIB). Now, if any PE gets a packet with a destination of subnet1, LSRs may simply forward IP packets by looking at labels and LFIB.

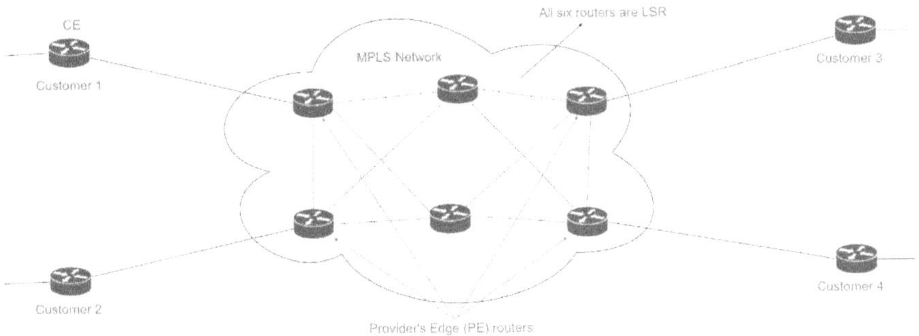

Very Small Aperture Terminal (VSAT): Very Small Aperture Terminal is referred to as VSAT. The advancement of technology and progress in satellite communication has made voice and data transmission more affordable for a wider variety of customers. The standard ground station size for VSAT is less than 2.4 metres in diameter. Even smaller dishes, with a diameter of little more than 1.5 m, are on the rise.

Very Small Aperture Terminal (VSAT) Structure: The graphic below depicts a VSAT network's fundamental architecture. A VSAT consists of two components: an outside transceiver with a clear line of sight to the satellite and an inside device that connects the transceiver to the final communications device, such a PC. An aerial satellite transponder receives or receives a signal from the transceiver. A ground station computer serves as the system's hub, sending and receiving messages to and from the satellite.

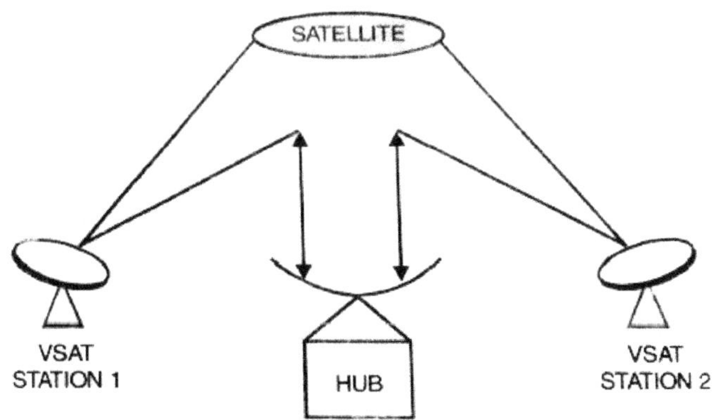

Network VSAT:

A star topology is created when each end user is connected to the hub station via a satellite. The hub oversees how the network is run as a whole. Each broadcast must first go to the hub station before being retransmitted via satellite to the other end user's VSAT for communication. The system is made up of a hub station that offers a broadcast facility to every VSAT in the network and the individual VSATs, which connect to the satellite via various multiple access modes.

A number of users may share the hub station, which is run by the service provider. Time-division multiplex (TDM) is the downlink mode of transmission from hub to VSAT, and the transmission can be broadcast for reception by all the VSATs in a network, or address coding can be used to direct messages to selected VSATs.

VSAT Network Architecture: VSAT systems can be implemented in three basic architectures,

- One-way implementation.
- Split-two-way implementation.

Two-way implementation.

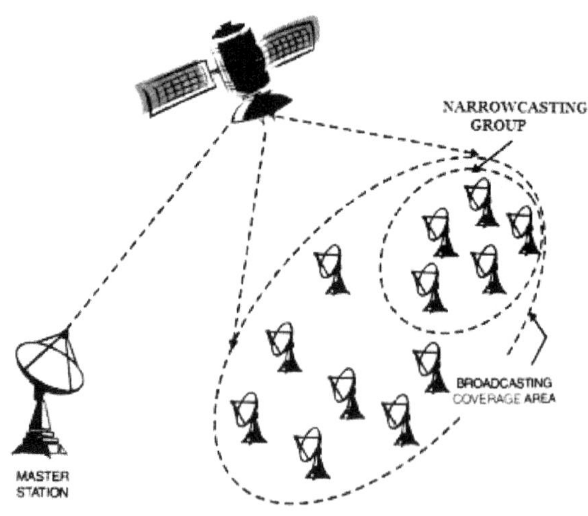

Schematic of one-way implementation

Split-Two-Way Implementation: This implementation is used when there is no normal return channel (E.g., with Ku band broadcast satellite service systems that carry Internet traffic). The relatively high capacity downlink stream is not complemented by an uplink capability from the user terminal. If the BSS downlink is used as the download channel from an internet service provider, the only option the user has for a return link is via another telecommunications channel, such as a standard telephone line. The Internet Protocol (IP) is therefore split between a satellite downlink (outbound) channel and a terrestrial telephone (inbound) channel: hence the term split IP for this implementation.

The advantage of this approach is that the VSAT terminal does not require a transmit capability, which significantly reduces its cost and complexity.

The disadvantage is that the telephone line connection must ususlly be through a modem, with a bet rate gencrally restricted to 56 kbps.

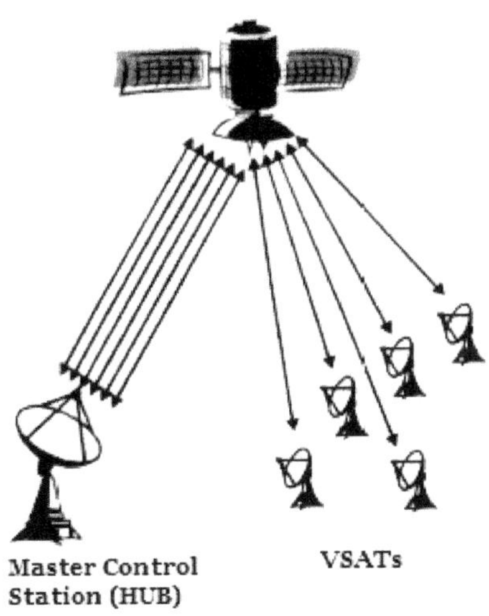

Split-Two-Way Implementation

Two Way Implementation: The service includes a return link so as to establish two-way communication over the same satellite, from the hub to the user and from the user back to the hub. Two topologies are implemented: Star topology and Mesh topology.

Star Topology: Here, all of the traffic is routed via the master control station, or hub. If a VSAT wishes to communicate with another VSAT, they have to go via the hub, thus necessitating a "double hop" link via the satellite. Since all of the traffic radiates at one time or another from the hub, this architecture is referred to as Star network.

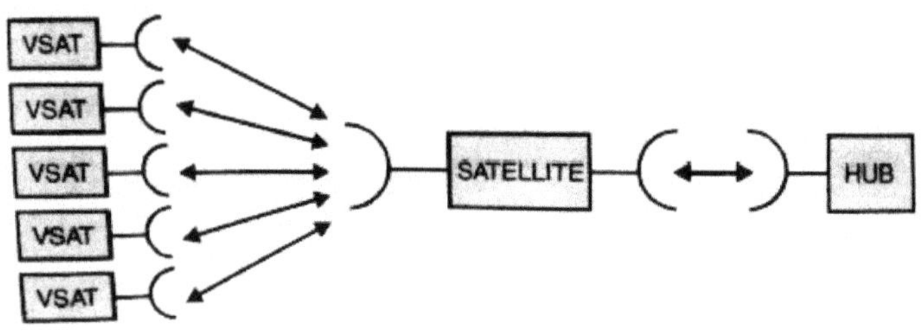

Star Topology

Mesh Topology: Here, each of the VSATs has the capability to directly communicate with any the other VSATs. The network control and the duties of the hub is either handled by one of the VSATs or the master control station functions are shared among the VSATs. Since the traffic can go to or from any of the VSATs, this architecture referred to as Mesh network.

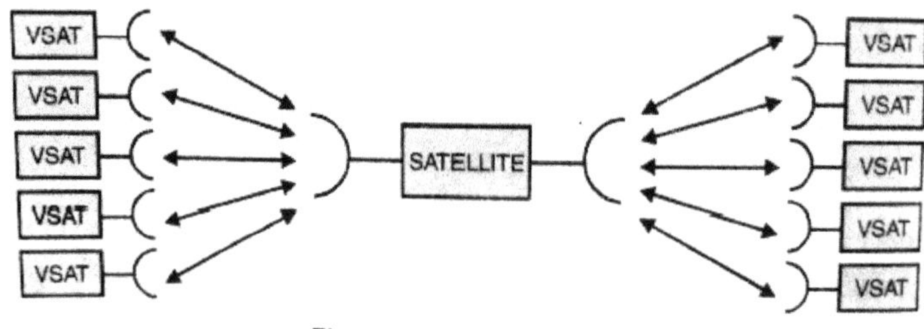

Mesh Topology

Specifications:

Some typical specifications of VSAT are:

- Antenna size: 1.2 m to 3.5 m
- Antenna gain: 40 dB
- Power uplink: 0.5-5 W

- G/T: 20 dB/°K

Typical specifications of Hub stations are:

- Antenna size: 3.5-10 m
- Antenna gain: 58 dB
- Power uplink: 50-200 W
- G/T: 30 dB/'K

Most VSAT systems operate in the Ku band (12-14 GHz) because it is less congested although there are some C-band systems in existance. For fixed area coverage by the satellite beam, the system performance is essentially independent of the carrier frequency. For fixed area coverage, the beamwidth and hence the ratio λ/D is a constant. The satellite antenna gain is therefore constant and for a given high power amplifier output, the satellite EIRP remains constant.

Applications of Very Small Aperture Terminal (VSAT) : Typical Applications of VSAT are:

- Computer communication
- Reservation system
- Database enquiries
- Billing system
- File transfer
- E-mail
- Video conferencing
- Stock control and management
- Credit card verification
- Point of sale transaction

Advantages of VSAT:

- Cost insensitive to distance.
- Easy for installation and maintenance.
- Flexibility.
- Upgradeable.
- Large number of VSAT networks can be integrated into the single network to provide cost effective expansion.

- Reliable service: 99.9% for data and 99.5% + for voice

Disadvantages of VSAT:

- High initial cost (hubs and basic elements must be placed before the services can be provided).
- Lack of adequate coverage in some parts of the world.
- Some service quantity limitations such as high signal delays (latency).
- Unavailability of direct links between various VSATs.
- Rain attenuation might affect the performance of VSAT communications under rainy conditions.

CHAPTER THREE

WIRELESS NETWORKS

Wi-Fi: The Wi-Fi Alliance, originally known as the Wireless Ethernet Compatibility Alliance, gave the title "Wi-Fi" to the communication standard for wireless networks that function as Local Area Networks without the use of cables or other forms of cabling. It is called WLAN. IEEE 802.11 is the communication standard. The Physical Data Link Layer powers Wi-Fi. All mobile computer devices today, including laptops, smartphones, digital cameras, and smart TVs, support Wi-Fi. Within a certain range, the access point, base station, client, or any client-to-client connection can create a Wi-Fi connection. The range is dependent on the router that transmits radio frequency through Wi-Fi. At the moment, these frequencies operate at 2.4 GHz and 5 GHz, respectively.

The Wi-Fi adaptor that is built into the laptop or mobile device determines whether it can use both bandwidths. Modern laptops and mobile devices can use both bandwidths. The standard band all devices support is 2.4 GHz. In order to spread the Wi-Fi signal, 2.4 GHz can cover a wide area, but since the frequency is low, the speed of the internet is less. In contrast, 5 GHz bandwidth can cover a smaller region, but because the frequency is higher, the speed is much higher.

Let's say, if there is an internet connection of 60 MB/s bandwidth, then for 2.4 GHz bandwidth, it provides approx 30 to 45 MB/s of bandwidth connection and for 5 GHz bandwidth, it provides approx 50 to 57 MB/s bandwidth.

Applications of Wi-Fi: Wi-Fi has many applications, it is used in all the sectors where a computer or any digital media is used, and also for entertainment Wi-Fi is used. Some of the applications are mentioned below –

- Accessing the Internet: We can wirelessly access the internet in any Wi-Fi-capable device.
- We can stream or cast audio or video wirelessly on any device using Wi-Fi for our entertainment.
- We can share files, data, etc between two or more computers or mobile phones using Wi-Fi, and the speed of the data transfer rate is also very high. Also, we can print any document using a Wi-Fi printer, which is very much used nowadays.
- We can use Wi-Fi as **HOTSPOTS** also, it points to Wireless Internet access for a particular range of areas. Using a Hotspot the owner of the main network connection can offer temporary network access to Wi-Fi-capable devices so that the users can use the network without knowing anything about the main network connection. Wi-Fi adapters mainly spread radio signals using the owner network connection to provide a hotspot.
- We may create straightforward wireless connections between two points using WLAN or Wi-Fi, which are referred to as point-to-point networks. This can be used to connect two places that are challenging to reach by wire, like two corporate buildings.
- One more important application is **VoWi-Fi**, which is known as **voice-over Wi-Fi**. Some years ago telecom companies introduced VoLTE (Voice over Long-Term Evolution). Nowadays they are introduced to VoWi-Fi, by which we can call anyone by using our home Wi-Fi network, only one thing is that the mobile needs to connect with the Wi-Fi. Then the voice is transferred using the Wi-Fi network instead of using the mobile SIM network, so the call quality is very good. Many mobile phones are already getting the support of VoWi-Fi.
- Workplace Wi-Fi: Wi-Fi is used to link every computer in an office. There are no complicated wiring issues with Wi-Fi. The network also has high speed. A project may be delivered to every member simultaneously via Wi-Fi in the form of an excel sheet, powerpoint, etc. For Wi-Fi, there is no network loss as in cable due to cable break.
- Also using Wi-Fi a whole city can provide network connectivity by deploying routers at a specific area to access the internet. Already schools, colleges, and universities are providing networks using Wi-Fi because of its flexibility.
- Wi-Fi is used as a positioning system also, by which we can detect the positions of Wi-Fi hotspots to identify a device location.

Types of Wi-Fi: Wi-Fi has several types of standards, which are discussed earlier, here just the name of the standards are defined.

- Wi-Fi-1 (802.11b) - 1999- This version has a link speed from 2Mb/s to 11 Mb/s over a 2.4 GHz frequency band.
- Wi-Fi-2 (802.11a) - 1999- After a month of release previous version, 802.11a was released and it provide up to 54 Mb/s link speed over 5 Ghz band.
- Wi-Fi-3 (802.11g) - 2003- In this version the speed was increased up to 54 to 108 Mb/s over 2.4 GHz

How does WiFi function? Since xWi-Fi is a wireless networking technology, it transmits networks via electromagnetic waves. We are aware that electromagnetic waves may be divided into various categories based on their frequency, including X-ray, gamma-ray, radio wave, microwave, etc. The radio frequency employed in Wi-Fi is one of these categories. There are three different mediums for transmitting Wi-Fi signals:

- **Base station network or an Ethernet(802.3) connection:** It is the main host network from where the network connection is provided to the router.
- **Access point or router:** it is a bridge between a wired network and a wireless network. It accepts a wired Ethernet connection and converts the wired connection to a wireless connection and spreads the connection as a radio wave.
- **Accessing devices:** It is our mobile, computer, etc from where we use the Wi-Fi and surfing internet.
- 802.11i- 2004- This is the same as 802.11g but only the security mechanism was increased in this version.
- 802.11e- 2004- This is also the same as 802.11g, only Voice over Wireless LAN and multimedia streaming are involved.
- Wi-Fi-4 (802.11n)- 2009- This version supports both 2.4 GHz and 5 GHz radio frequency and it offers up to 72 to 600 Mb/s speed.
- Wi-Fi-5 (802.11ac)- 2014- It supports a speed of 1733 Mb/s in the 5 GHz band.
- A new version will release in 2020 named 802.11ax developed by **Huawei**, which can support, a maximum of 3.5 Gb/s. it will know **Wi-Fi 6.**

How does Wi-Fi work?

Since Wi-Fi is a wireless networking technology, it transmits networks via electromagnetic waves. We are aware that electromagnetic waves may be divided into various categories based on their frequency, including X-ray, gamma-ray, radio wave, microwave, etc. The radio frequency employed in Wi-Fi is one of these categories. There are three different mediums for transmitting Wi-Fi signals:

- **Base station network or an Ethernet(802.3) connection:** It is the main host network from where the network connection is provided to the router.
- **Access point or router:** it is a bridge between a wired network and a wireless network. It accepts a wired Ethernet connection and converts the wired connection to a wireless connection and spreads the connection as a radio wave.
- **Accessing devices:** It is our mobile, computer, etc from where we use the Wi-Fi and surfing the internet.

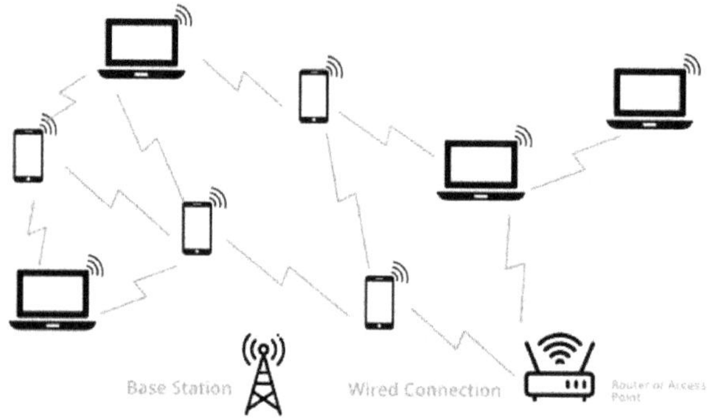

Working of Wi-Fi: All the electronics devices read data in binary form, also router or our devices, here routers provide radio waves and those waves are receive by our devices and read the waves in binary form. We all know how a wave looks like, the upper pick of the wave is known as 1 and the lower pick of the wave is known as 0 in binary. Like below:

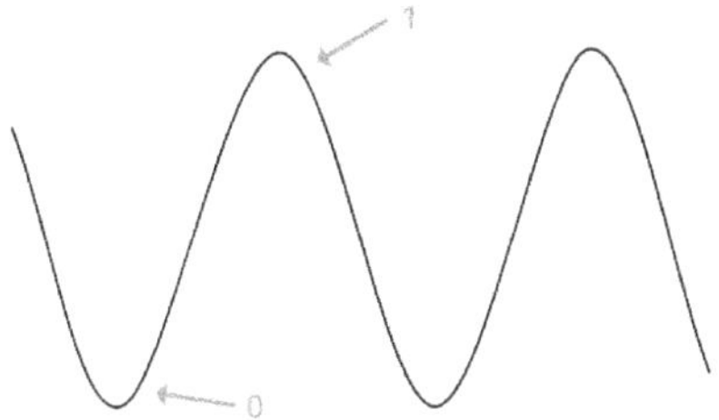

Data transmission

Some more terminologies

- **SSID (Service Set Identifier):** It is a 32 character name that identifies the Wi-Fi network and differentiates one Wi-Fi from another Wi-Fi. All the devices are attempting to connect a particular SSID. Simply, SSID is the name of the wireless network.
- **WPA-PSK (Wi-Fi Protected Access- Pre-Shared Key):** It is a program developed by the Wi-Fi Alliance Authority to secure wireless networks with the use of Pre-Shared Key(PSK) authentication. WPA has 3 types, such as WPA. WPA2, WPA3. It is a way of encrypting the Wi-Fi signal to protect from unwanted users.
- Wi-Fi uses **Ad-Hoc** networks to transmit. It is a point-to-point network without any interface.

How signals are reached to our devices?

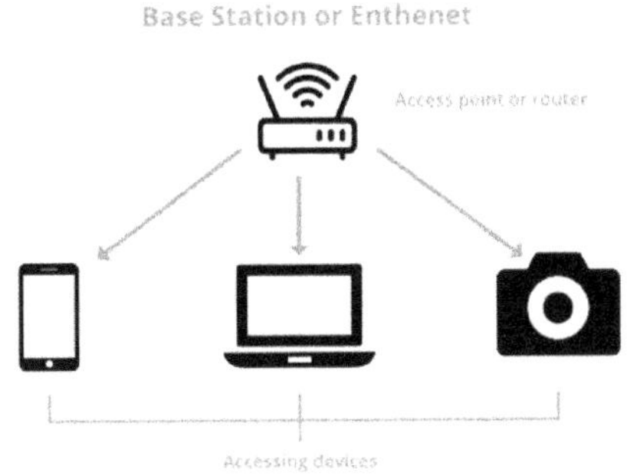

Base Station

Advantages of Wi-Fi:

- It is a flexible network connection, no wiring complexities. Can be accessed from anywhere in the Wi-Fi range.
- It does not require regulatory approval for individual users.
- It is salable, can be expanded by using Wi-Fi Extenders.
- It can be set up in an easy and fast way. Just need to configure the SSID and Password.
- Security in a high in Wi-Fi network, its uses **WPA** encryption to encrypt radio signals.
- It is also lower in cost.
- It also can provide Hotspots.
- it supports roaming also.

Disadvantages of Wi-Fi:

- Power consumption is high while using Wi-Fi in any device which has a battery, such as mobile, laptops, etc.
- Many times there may be some security problems happening even it has encryption. Such as many times has known devices become unknown to the router, Wi-Fi can be hacked also.
- Speed is slower than a direct cable connection.
- It has lower radiation like cell phones, so it can harm humans.
- Wi-Fi signals may be affected by climatic conditions like thunderstorms.
- Unauthorized access to Wi-Fi can happen because it does not have a firewall.
- To use Wi-Fi we need a router, which needs a power source, so at the time of power cut, we cannot access the internet.

WiMax: WiMax stands for **Worldwide Inter-operability for Microwave Access.** This technology is based on IEEE 802.16. It is used to provide higher data rates with increased coverage. It is based on MAN (Metropolitan Area Network) technology. Its range is upto 50 Km. It may provide speed upto 70 Mbps and it can operate in Non-Line-of-Sight. This technology is fast, convenient and cost effective.

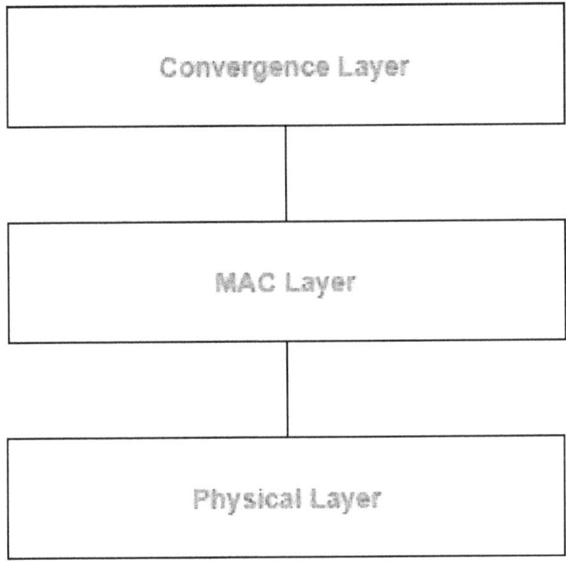

Architecture

1. **Physical Layer:**This layer controls bit transmission and reception as well as the encoding and decoding of signals. It transforms MAC layer frames into sent signals. Modulation schemes which are used on this layer includes: QPSK, QAM-16 and QAM-64.
2. **MAC Layer:**This layer serves as an interface for the WiMax protocol stack's convergence layer and physical layer. It uses CSMA/CA and offers point-to-multipoint communication (Carrier Sense Multiple Access with Collision Avoidance).
3. **Convergence Layer:**
   This layer provides the information of the external network. It accepts higher layer protocol data unit (PDU) and converts it to lower layer PDU. It provides functions depending upon the service being used.

Applications:

- Video streaming
- VoIP
- Video Conference

- E-Learning

Cellular Phone Technologies – GSM: GSM stands for **Global System for Mobile Communication.** GSM is an open and digital cellular technology used for mobile communication. It uses 4 different frequency bands of 850 MHz, 900 MHz, 1800 MHz and 1900 MHz . It uses the combination of FDMA and TDMA. This article includes all the concepts of GSM architecture and how it works.

GSM is having 4 different sizes of cells are used in GSM :

1. Macro : In this size of cell, Base Station antenna is installed.
2. Micro : In this size of cell, antenna height is less than the average roof level.
3. Pico : Small cells' diameter of few meters.
4. Umbrella : It covers the shadowed (Fill the gaps between cells) regions.

Features of GSM are :

1. Supports international roaming
2. Clear voice clarity
3. Ability to support multiple handheld devices.
4. Spectral / frequency efficiency
5. Low powered handheld devices.
6. Ease of accessing network
7. International ISDN compatibility.

GSM is nothing but a larger system which is divided into further 3 subsystems.

1. **BSS :** BSS stands for Base Station Subsystem. BSS handles traffic and signaling between a mobile phone and the network switching subsystem. BSS having two components **BTS** and **BSC.**
2. **NSS :** NSS stands for Network and Switching Subsystem. NSS is the core network of GSM. That carried out call and mobility management functions for mobile phone present in network. NSS have different components like **VLR, HLR** and **EIR.**
3. **OSS :** OSS stands for Operating Subsystem. OSS is a functional entity which the network operator monitor and control the system. **OMC** is

the part of OSS. Purpose of OSS is to offer the customer cost-effective support for all GSM related maintenance services.

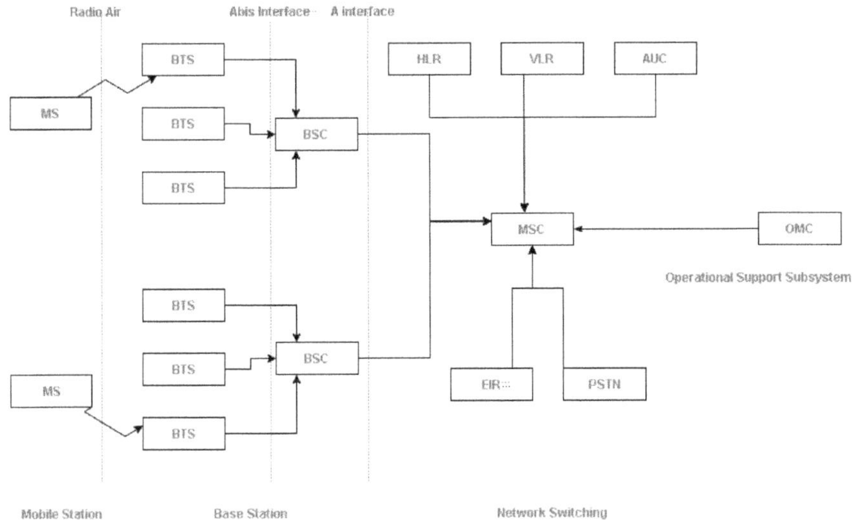

Suppose there are 3 Mobile stations that are connected with the tower and that tower is connected to BTS through TRX, then further connected to BSC and MSC. Let's understand the functionality of different components.

1. MS: Mobile System is referred to as MS. MS consists of the user tools and software required for connecting to a mobile network. Mobile Equipment (ME) + Subscriber Identity Module makes up a mobile station (MS) (SIM). Currently, the tower to which these mobile stations are attached is linked to the BTS by TRX. A transceiver called a TRX has a transmitter and a receiver. The transceiver may broadcast and receive data in two different ways.

2. BTS: BTS stands for Base Transceiver Station which facilitates wireless communication between a user equipment and a network. Every tower has BTS.

3. BSC: BSC stands for Base Station Controller. BSC has multiple BTS. You can consider the BSC as a local exchange of your area which has multiple towers and multiple towers that have BTS.

4. MSC: MSC, or the mobile switching centre, stands for. Call setup, call release, and routing are examples of communication switching functions that are related to MSC. Call tracing, and call forwarding all functions are performed at the MSC level. MSC is having further components like VLR, HLR, AUC, EIR, and PSTN.

- **VLR:** VLR stands for Visitor Location Register. VLR is a database that contains the exact location of all mobile subscribers currently present in the service area of MSC. If you are going from one state to another state then your entry is marked in the database of VLR.
- **HLR:** HLR stands for Home Location Register. HLR is a database containing pertinent data regarding subscribers authorized to use a GSM network.. If you purchase a SIM card from the HLR. HLR is like a home that contains all data like your ID proof, which plan you are taking, which caller tune you are using etc.
- **OMC:** OMC stands for Operation Maintenance Center. OMC monitor and maintain the performance of each MS, BSC, and MSC within a GSM system.
- **AUC:** AUC stands for Authentication Center. AUC authenticates the mobile subscriber that wants to connect to the network.
- **EIR:** EIR stands for Equipment Identity Register. EIR is a database that keeps the record of all allowed or banned in the network. If you are banned from the network you can't enter the network, and you can't make calls.
- **PSTN:** Public Switched Telephone Network is referred to as PSTN. PSTN and MSC are linked. Initially, PSTN was a fixed-line, analogue telephone system network. Its primary network is now nearly totally digital and covers landline telephones as well as mobile and other networks. The older landlines that we still have at home are simply PSTN. Three subsystems BSS, NSS, and OSS are connected with each other via some interfaces. Total of three interfaces are there:

    - **Air Interface:** Air interface is also known as UM interface. The interface between MS and BTS is called as UM interface because it is mobile analog to the U interface of ISDN.
    - **Abis Interface:** It is a BSS internal interface linking with BTS and BSC.
    - **An interface:** It provides communication between BSS and MSC. Hence, this is the complete architecture and functionalities of GSM components.

CDMA - Code Division Multiple Access is what it stands for. QUALCOMM is the company behind CDMA. The 800 megahertz (MHz) and 1.9 gigahertz (GHz) bands of UHF (ultra-high-frequency) cellular phone networks employ this technology. In essence, it is a type of complexing that permits several signals to duplicate a single transmission channel without using all of the available bandwidth. It utilises digital-to-analog conversion (ADC) technology. Binary components are initially created by digitising the audio input.

Advantages:

- It offers increased cellular communication security, by not being easily decryptable.
- Consumes less power and gives better coverage.
- No synchronization is required.
- It is relatively easier to add many numbers of users.
- It has a very high spectral capacity so it can accommodate more users per MHz of bandwidth.
- The dropouts occur only when the phone is twice as far from the base station.

Disadvantages:

- The CDMA system is very complicated.
- With the increase in the number of users, the overall quality of services decreases.
- The time that is required for sending and receiving data and signals is huge.
- Doesn't work in international roaming.
- It is costly.

Applications:

- The most important and most familiar usage of CDMA is linked with GPS (Global Positioning System).
- It is used for over-the-air activation and also for personal communication services.
- It is used in Bluetooth, phone companies, radar and navigation systems, and wireless laptop modems, and is also used for subscriber access

control.

What is the importance of CDMA in today's cellular world?

The smooth transition to digital standards is crucial, and progressing toward 4G technology is compatible with CDMA technology. It is also seen as a substitute for TDMA (Time Division Multiple Access), a digital modulation method used in mobile radio and digital cellular phone communication. The fastest and safest methods of data sharing, such 3G, are provided by CDMA, which is regarded as the highest wireless communication standard. Numerous 3G cellular telecommunications networks have used CDMA technology because it has a number of benefits. Additionally, a terminal may easily interact with two base stations at once when employing CDMA technology. It emerges as a winner in the battle of wireless technology and services. It allows far greater development and the use of broadband devices such as wireless laptop modems, GPS system units, and other devices. CDMA provides high-speed push-to-talk and push-to-email services which gives mobiles the ability to be used as a walky-talky device. Therefore, it is good for business purposes too.

0th Generation:

- Pre-cell phone mobile telephony technology, such as radio telephones some had in cars before the arrival of cell phones.
- Communication was possible through voice only.
- These mobile telephones were usually mounted in cars or trucks.

1G (1st Generation):

- First-time calling was introduced in mobile systems.
- It used analog signals.
- It used an FDD scheme and typically allocated a bandwidth of 25 Mhz.
- The coverage area was small.
- No roaming support between various operators.
- Low sound quality.
- Speed:- 2.4 kbps.

2G (2nd Generation) :

- Shifted from analog to digital.

- It supported voice and SMS both.
- Supported all 4 sectors of the wireless industry namely Digital cellular, Mobile Data, PCS, WLAN,
- Moderate mobile data service.
- 2G WLAN provided a high data rate & large area coverage.
- Speed:- 64 kbps.

2.5G- 2.5G Came after **2G** which used the concept of GPRS. Streaming was also introduced and mail services too. Then came **2.75G** or EDGE which was faster in providing services than 2.5G. It gave faster internet speed up to 128kbps and also used edge connection.

3G (3rd Generation) :

- The Internet system was improved.
- Better system and capacity.
- Offers high-speed wireless internet.
- The connection used was UMTS and WCMA.
- Speed:- 2mbps.

4G (4th Generation) :

- IP-based protocols.
- LTE (Long term evaluation) was mainly for the internet.
- Vo-LTE (Voice over LTE) is for both voice and the internet.
- Freedom and flexibility to select any desired service with reasonable QoS.
- High usability.
- Supports multimedia service at a low transmission cost.
- HD Quality Streaming.
- Speed:-100mbps.

5G(5th Generation):

- It is yet to come in many countries but here are some notable points about 5G.
- Higher data rates.
- Connectivity will be more fast and more secure,
- Data Latency will be reduced to a great level.

- Massive network capacity.
- It is 30 times faster than 4G.
- There would be more flexibility in the network.

4G LTE Performance Monitoring Complexity: 4G LTE network environment is complex, consisting of

- **the radio access network (RAN) segment** with
  - devices for handling data translation and signaling from the wireless infrastructure,
  - high-capacity cell site routers.
- **the backhaul segment** with many large, point-to-point routers and some times microwave or millimeter-wave wireless links
- **the packet core** where resources such as packet gateways, and authentication and authorization systems are located.
- **the data centers** housing resources such as rewalls, load balancers, and internal LAN switches.
- **the IP multimedia subsystem (IMS) core**, where services like streaming video and visual voice mail reside on large, strategically located server clusters.

CHAPTER FOUR

Introduction to Network Security

Virtual LAN (VLAN):

With the help of the virtual LAN (VLAN) idea, layer 2 devices may be divided logically (data link layer). In general, layer 3 devices split the broadcast domain, however switches can also divide the broadcast domain using the VLAN concept.

A broadcast domain is a section of a network where every device within the same broadcast domain will receive a packet that is broadcast there. All broadcast packets will be received by the devices in the same broadcast domain, but only switches may receive them because routers don't forward out broadcast packets. Inter Vlan routing is required to forward packets to various VLANs (from one VLAN to another) or the broadcast domain. Different small-size sub-networks are built with VLAN, which are quite simple to manage.

VLAN ranges –

- **VLAN 0, 4095:** These are reserved VLAN which cannot be seen or used.
- **VLAN 1:** It is the default VLAN of switches. By default, all switch ports are in VLAN. This VLAN can't be deleted or edit but can be used.
- **VLAN 2-1001:** This is a normal VLAN range. We can create, edit and delete these VLAN.
- **VLAN 1002-1005:** These are CISCO defaults for fddi and token rings. These VLAN can't be deleted.
- **Vlan 1006-4094:** This is the extended range of Vlan.

Configuration –

We can simply create VLANs by simply assigning the vlan-id and Vlan name.

#switch1(config)#vlan 2

#switch1(config-vlan)#vlan accounts

Here, 2 is the Vlan I'd and accounts is the Vlan name. Now, we assign Vlan to the switch ports.e.g-

- Switch(config)#int fa0/0
- Switch(config-if)#switchport mode access
- Switch(config-if)#switchport access Vlan 2
- Also, switchport range can be assigned to required vlans.
- Switch(config)#int range fa0/0-2
- Switch(config-if)#switchport mode access
- Switch(config-if) #switchport access Vlan 2

By this, switchport fa0/0, fa0/1, fa0-2 will be assigned Vlan 2.

Example –

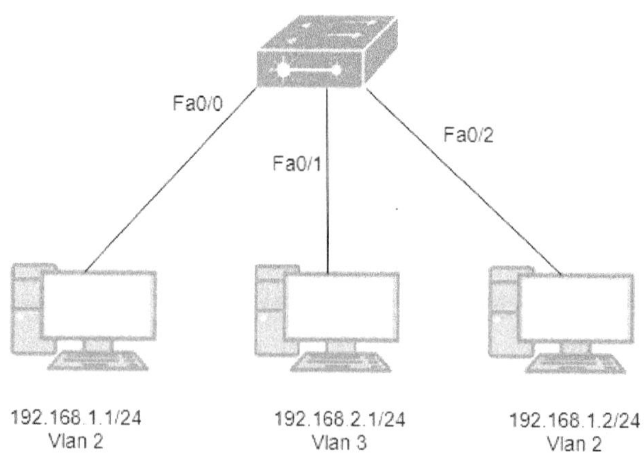

Assigning IP address 192.168.1.1/24, 192.168.1.2/24 and 192.168.2.1/ 24 to the PC's. Now, we will create Vlan 2 and 3 on switch.

- Switch(config)#vlan 2
- Switch(config)#vlan 3

We have made VLANs but the most important part is to assign switch ports to the VLANs.

- Switch(config)#int fa0/0
- Switch(config-if)#switchport mode access
- Switch(config-if) #switchport access Vlan 2
- Switch(config)#int fa0/1
- Switch(config-if)#switchport mode access
- Switch(config-if) #switchport access Vlan 3
- Switch(config)#int fa0/2
- Switch(config-if)#switchport mode access
- Switch(config-if) #switchport access Vlan 2

As seen, we have assigned Vlan 2 to fa0/0, fa0/2, and Vlan 3 to fa0/1.

Types of connections in VLAN –

Devices can be linked to a VLAN in three different ways, depending on whether they are VLAN-aware (devices that understand VLAN formats and VLAN membership) or VLAN-unaware (devices that don't understand VLAN formats and VLAN membership).

1. **Trunk Link** – All connected devices to a trunk link must be VLAN-aware. All frames on this should have a special header attached to it called tagged frames.
2. **Access link** – It connects VLAN-unaware devices to a VLAN-aware bridge. All frames on the access link must be untagged.
3. **Hybrid link** – It is a combination of the Trunk link and Access link. Here both VLAN-unaware and VLAN-aware devices are attached and they can have both tagged and untagged frames.

Advantages –

1. **Performance** –There is a lot of broadcast and multicast traffic on the network. VLAN lessens the necessity of sending such traffic to pointless locations. For instance, if a broadcast or multicast packet is meant for two users, but ten devices are present in the same broadcast domain, all of them would get it, wasting bandwidth. However, if we create VLANs, the broadcast or multicast packet will only be transmitted to the intended users.

2. **Formation of virtual groups –**
   As there are different departments in every organization namely sales, finance etc., VLANs can be very useful in order to group the devices logically according to their departments.
3. **Security –**
   In the same network, sensitive data can be broadcast which can be accessed by the outsider but by creating VLAN, we can control broadcast domains, set up firewalls, restrict access. Also, VLANs can be used to inform the network manager of an intrusion. Hence, VLANs greatly enhance network security.
4. **Flexibility –**
   VLAN provide flexibility to add, remove the number of host we want.
5. **Cost reduction –**
   VLANs can be used to create broadcast domains which eliminate the need for expensive routers.
   By using Vlan, the number of small size broadcast domain can be increased which are easy to handle as compared to a bigger broadcast domain.

VPN:

The term "VPN" refers to a virtual private network. Through the use of a virtual private network (VPN), a secure and encrypted connection may be established across a less secure network, such the internet. A virtual private network (VPN) uses a public network, such the internet, to extend a private network. The term solely alludes to the fact that it is a virtual "private network," meaning that a user may join a local network while seated at a distance. To provide a secure connection, tunnelling technologies are used.

Lets understand VPN by an example:

Consider a scenario in which a bank's corporate headquarters is located in Washington, USA. The local network in this office contains, let's say, 100 machines. Let's say the bank has locations in Mumbai, India, and Tokyo, Japan. A leased line between the branches and the head office was the conventional means of creating a secure connection between head office and branch, but this was a highly expensive and difficult task. VPN enables us to successfully resolve this problem.

The situation is described below:

- All 100 hundred computers of the corporate office at Washington are connected to the VPN server(which is a well-configured server containing a public IP address and a switch to connect all computers present in the local network i.e. in US head office).
- The person sitting in the Mumbai office connects to The VPN server using a dial-up window and the VPN server returns an IP address that belongs to the series of IP addresses belonging to a local network of the corporate office.
- This person from the Mumbai branch becomes local to the head office and information can be shared securely over the public internet.
- So this is the intuitive way of extending the local network even across the geographical borders of the country.

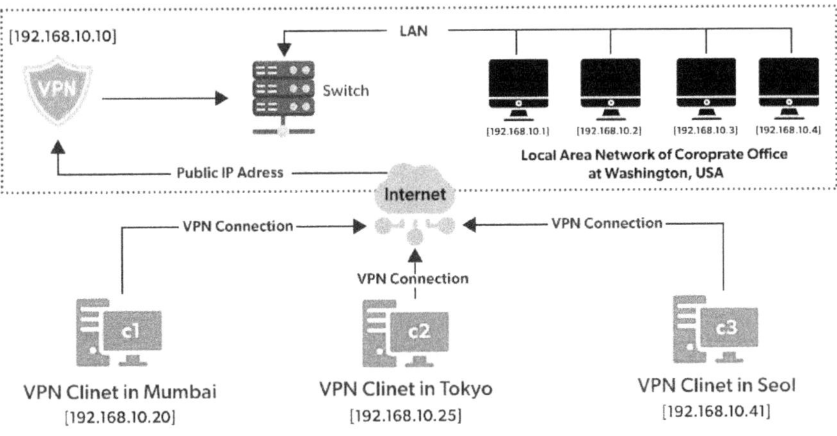

VPN is well exploited all across the globe: We will explain to you with an example. Suppose we are using smartphones regularly. Spotify-a Swedish music app which is not active in India But we are making full use of it sitting in India. So how ?? VPN can be used to camouflage our geolocation.

- Suppose the Ip address is 101.22.23.3 which belongs to India. That's why our device is not able to access the Spotify music app.
- But the magic begins when we used the Psiphon app which is an android app and is used to change the device IP address to the IP address of the location we want(say US where Spotify works in a seamless manner).

- The IP address is changed using VPN technology. Basically what happens is that your device will connect to a VPN server of the respective country that you have entered in your location textbox of the Psiphon app and now you will inherit a new IP from this server.

Now we typed "what is my IP address"? Amazingly the IP address changed to 45.79.66.125 which belongs to the USA And since Spotify works well in the US, so we can use it now being in India (virtually in the USA). Is not that good? obviously, it is very useful.

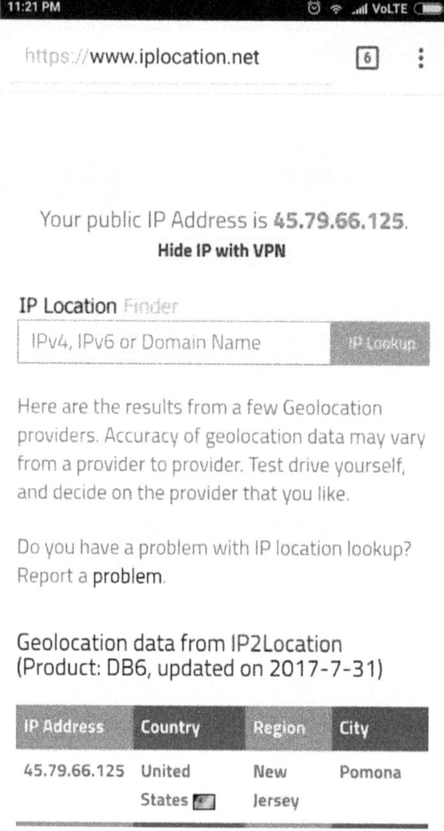

IP address changed to an IP address belonging to USA

- VPN also ensures security by providing an encrypted tunnel between client and VPN server.

- VPN is used to bypass many blocked sites.
- VPN facilitates Anonymous browsing by hiding your ip address.
- Also, most appropriate Search engine optimization(SEO) is done by analyzing the data from VPN providers which provide country-wise stats of browsing a particular product. This method of SEO is used widely my many internet marketing managers to form new strategies.
- A firewall is a network security device, either hardware or software-based, which monitors all incoming and outgoing traffic and based on a defined set of security rules it accepts, rejects or drops that specific traffic.
- **Accept :** allow the traffic
  Reject : block the traffic but reply with an "unreachable error"
  Drop : block the traffic with no reply

A firewall establishes a barrier between secured internal networks and outside untrusted network, such as the Internet.

VPN and its legality

Using VPN is legal in most of the countries,. The legality of using a VPN service depends on the country and its geopolitical relations with another country as well. A reliable and secure VPN is always legal if you are not intended to use it for any illegal activities like committing fraud online, cyber theft, or in some countries downloading copyrighted content.

China has decided to block all VPN(Virtual private network)s by next year, as per the report of Bloomberg. Many Chinese Internet users use VPNs to privately access websites that are blocked under China's so-called "great firewall". This is done to avoid any information leakage to rival countries and so as to tighten the information security.

Firewall: A firewall is a network security device, either hardware or software-based, which monitors all incoming and outgoing traffic and based on a defined set of security rules it accepts, rejects or drops that specific traffic.

Accept : allow the traffic
Reject : block the traffic but reply with an "unreachable error"
Drop : block the traffic with no reply

A firewall establishes a barrier between secured internal networks and outside untrusted network, such as the Internet.

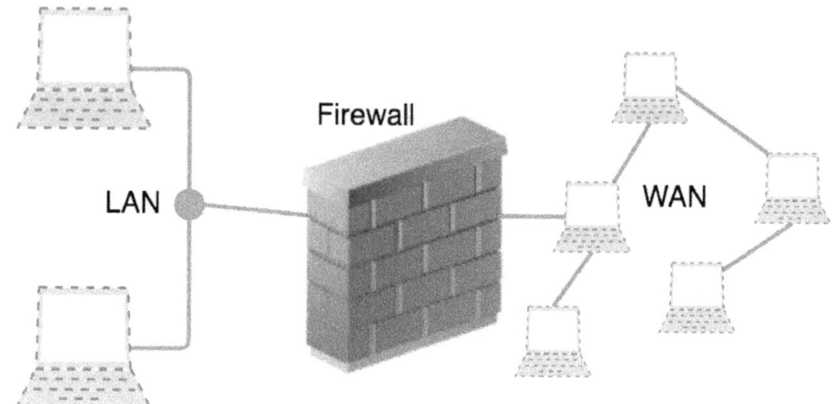

FIREWALL

History and Need for Firewall: Access Control Lists (ACLs) kept networks secure before firewalls by being located on routers. ACLs are rules that specify whether a given IP address should be allowed or prohibited access to the network.

ACLs, however, are unable to identify the type of packets they are preventing. Additionally, ACL by itself is unable to prevent threats from entering the network. Hence, the Firewall was introduced.

Organizations can no longer avoid having Internet access. However, having Internet connectivity helps the company and allows external users to communicate with the internal network of the company. This puts the organisation in danger. We require a Firewall to protect the internal network from illegitimate traffic.

How Firewall Works: Network traffic is compared by firewalls with the rule set specified in their table. As soon as the rule is matched, the network traffic is subjected to the associated action. As an instance, one rule states that no employee from the HR department may access the data on the code server, but a different rule states that the system administrator may access the data from both the HR and technical departments. Rules can be set up on the firewall depending on organisational requirements and security guidelines

Network traffic can be either outgoing or incoming from the viewpoint of a server. For each of these situations, the firewall maintains an own set of rules. Most of the outgoing traffic, which came from the server, was permitted to proceed. To increase security and stop undesirable communication, it is still always preferable to define a rule for outbound traffic. Different rules are applied to oncoming traffic. One of these three main Transport Layer protocols—TCP, UDP, or ICMP—makes up the majority of traffic that enters the firewall. These kinds are all addressed at both their source and destination. TCP and UDP both have port numbers. To identify the purpose of a packet, ICMP utilises a type code rather than a port number.

Default policy: It is quite challenging to explicitly cover every firewall rule that might exist. This necessitates that the firewall always have a default policy. Action is the only component of default policy (accept, reject or drop).

Let's say the firewall has no rules about SSH connections to the server. It will thus adhere to the default policy. Any computer outside of your business can connect to the server using SSH if the firewall's default policy is configured to accept. Therefore, it is usually a good practise to set the default policy to drop (or reject).

Generation of Firewall: Firewalls can be categorized based on its generation.

- **First Generation- Packet Filtering Firewall :** By monitoring incoming and outgoing packets and deciding whether to let them through or not depending on source and destination IP addresses, protocols, and ports, packet filtering firewalls are used to restrict access to networks. It examines transport protocol layer traffic (but mainly uses first 3 layers). Packet firewalls treat each packet in isolation. They have no ability to tell whether a packet is part of an existing stream of traffic. Only It can allow or deny the packets based on unique packet headers.
- Packet filtering firewall maintains a filtering table which decides whether the packet will be forwarded or discarded. From the given filtering table, the packets will be Filtered according to following rules:

	Source IP	Dest. IP	Source Port	Dest. Port	Action
1	192.168.21.0	--	--	--	deny
2	--	--	--	23	deny
3	--	192.168.21.3	--	--	deny
4	--	192.168.21.0	--	>1023	Allow

Sample Packet Filter Firewall Rule

1. Incoming packets from network 192.168.21.0 are blocked.
2. Incoming packets destined for internal TELNET server (port 23) are blocked.
3. Incoming packets destined for host 192.168.21.3 are blocked.
4. All well-known services to the network 192.168.21.0 are allowed.

- **Second Generation- Stateful Inspection Firewall** : Stateful firewalls (which carry out Stateful Packet Inspection) are more effective than packet filtering firewalls because they can tell the connection status of a packet. It monitors the status of network connections, including TCP streams, that pass through it. As a result, the filtering choices would take into account both the packet history in the state table and the set criteria.
- Note: Application layer firewalls can also be used as Network Address Translator(NAT).
- **Next Generation Firewalls (NGFW)** : In order to prevent contemporary security breaches such advanced malware assaults and application-layer attacks, next generation firewalls are being used. To defend the network from these contemporary dangers, NGFW includes Deep Packet Inspection, Application Inspection, SSL/SSH Inspection, and many more features.
- **Third Generation- Application Layer Firewall** : Any OSI layer, up to the application layer, can have packets inspected and filtered by an application layer firewall. It can determine when individual applications and protocols (like HTTP and FTP) are being abused and block specific

material as well.

In other words, hosts that operate proxy servers are Application layer firewalls. Each packet must transit through the proxy in a proxy firewall in order to establish a direct connection between either side of the firewall. Depending on previously established restrictions, it might permit or prevent traffic.

- **Next Generation Firewalls (NGFW)** : Next Generation Firewalls are being deployed these days to stop modern security breaches like advance malware attacks and application-layer attacks. NGFW consists of Deep Packet Inspection, Application Inspection, SSL/SSH inspection and many functionalities to protect the network from these modern threats.
- **Types of Firewall:** Firewalls are generally of two types: Host-based and Network-based.

1. **Host- based Firewalls :** Each network node has a host-based firewall installed, which regulates all incoming and outgoing packets. It is a piece of software—or a group of software—that is included with the operating system. Host-based firewalls are needed because network firewalls cannot provide protection inside a trusted network. Host firewall protects each host from attacks and unauthorized access.
2. **Network-based Firewalls :** Network firewall function on network level. In other words, these firewalls filter all incoming and outgoing traffic across the network. It protects the internal network by filtering the traffic using rules defined on the firewall. A Network firewall might have two or more network interface cards (NICs). A network-based firewall is usually a dedicated system with proprietary software installed. Both types of firewall have their own advantages.

IPS:

The terms intrusion detection and prevention system and intrusion prevention system are interchangeable. It is a network security tool that checks system or network activity for suspicious behaviour. The main duties of intrusion prevention systems are to spot harmful behaviour, gather data on it, report it, and make an effort to block or halt it.

Because both IPS and IDS monitor network traffic and system operations for malicious behaviour, intrusion prevention systems are thought of as an addition to intrusion detection systems (IDS).

Typically, IPS create reports, collect data pertaining to observed events, and alert security administrators to significant observed occurrences. Many IPS also have the ability to react to a danger by making an effort to stop it from happening. They employ a variety of reaction strategies, including the IPS blocking the attack directly, altering the security context, or altering the assault's content.

Classification of Intrusion Prevention System (IPS):

Intrusion Prevention System (IPS) is classified into 4 types:

1. **Network-based intrusion prevention system (NIPS):**
   It monitors the entire network for suspicious traffic by analyzing protocol activity.
2. **Wireless intrusion prevention system (WIPS):**
   It monitors a wireless network for suspicious traffic by analyzing wireless networking protocols.
3. **Network behavior analysis (NBA):**
   It examines network traffic to identify threats that generate unusual traffic flows, such as distributed denial of service attacks, specific forms of malware and policy violations.
4. **Host-based intrusion prevention system (HIPS):**
   It is an inbuilt software package which operates a single host for doubtful activity by scanning events that occur within that host.

Comparison of Intrusion Prevention System (IPS) Technologies:

The Table below indicates various kinds of IPS Technologies:

IPS Technology Type	Types of Malicious Activity Detected	Scope per Sensor	Strengths
Network-Based	Network, transport, and application TCP/IP layer activity	Multiple network subnets and groups of hosts	Only IDPS which can analyze the widest range of application protocols;
Wireless	Wireless protocol activity; unauthorized wireless local area networks (WLAN) in use	Multiple WLANs and groups of wireless clients	Only IDPS able to predict wireless protocol activity
NBA	Network, transport, and application TCP/IP layer activity that causes anomalous network flows	Multiple network subnets and groups of hosts	Typically, more effective than the others at identifying reconnaissance scanning and DoS attacks, and at reconstructing major malware infections
Host-Based	Host application and operating system (OS) activity; network, transport, and application TCP/IP layer activity	Individual host	Can analyze activity that was transferred in end-to-end encrypted communications

Detection Method of Intrusion Prevention System (IPS):

1. **Signature-based detection:**
   Signature-based IDS operates packets in the network and compares with pre-built and preordained attack patterns known as signatures.
2. **Statistical anomaly-based detection:**
   Anomaly based IDS monitors network traffic and compares it against an established baseline. The baseline will identify what is normal for that network and what protocols are used. However, It may raise a false alarm if the baselines are not intelligently configured.

3. **Stateful protocol analysis detection:**
   This IDS method recognizes divergence of protocols stated by comparing observed events with pre-built profiles of generally accepted definitions of not harmful activity.

Comparison of IPS with IDS:

The main difference between Intrusion Prevention System (IPS) with Intrusion Detection Systems (IDS) are:

1. Intrusion prevention systems are placed in-line and are able to actively prevent or block intrusions that are detected.
2. IPS can take such actions as sending an alarm, dropping detected malicious packets, resetting a connection or blocking traffic from the offending IP address.
3. IPS also can correct cyclic redundancy check (CRC) errors, defragment packet streams, mitigate TCP sequencing issues and clean up unwanted transport and network layer options.

Proxy Servers: The proxy server is a computer connected to the internet that receives inbound requests from clients and sends them on to the target server. Between the end user and the internet, it functions as a gateway. It has a distinct IP address. It isolates the web server and client systems from the global network. With another way of putting it, we can say that the proxy server enables us to visit any websites with a different IP address. Between users and the targeted websites or servers, it acts as a middleman. In response to user queries, it gathers and provides information. A proxy server's inability to encrypt communications is its most crucial flaw.

There are two main purposes of proxy servers:

- To keep the system behind it anonymous.
- To speed up access to a resource through caching.

Mechanism of Proxy Server: The following figure depicts the mechanism of the proxy server.

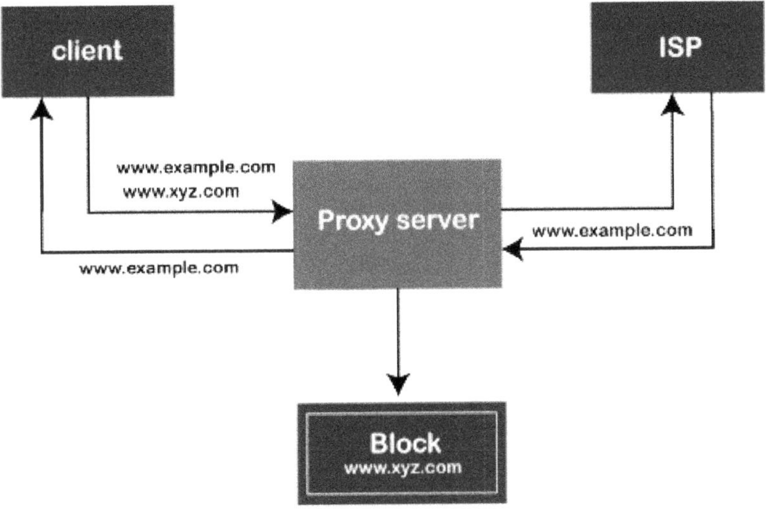

Mechanism of Proxy Server

The proxy server accepts the request from the client and produces a response based on the following conditions:

1. If the requested data or page already exists in the local cache, the proxy server itself provides the required retrieval to the client.
2. If the requested data or page does not exist in the local cache, the proxy server forwards that request to the destination server.
3. The proxy servers transfer the replies to the client and also being cached to them.

Therefore, it can be said that the proxy server acts as a client as well as the server.

Communication without proxy server

Communication with proxy server

Types of Proxy Servers

There are many types of proxy servers available. The two most common types of proxy servers are **forward** and **reverse proxy servers**. The other proxy server has its own feature and advantages. Let's discuss each in detail.

1. Open or Forward Proxy Server: The consumer is able to reach this sort of intermediary worker the most frequently. Any type of intermediary that accepts requests from web clients and then browses locations to acquire the requested information is referred to as an open or forward proxy server. After collecting the data from the sites, it forwards the data to the internet users directly. It avoids the government-built barrier. The following image shows forward proxy configuration.

2. Reverse Proxy Server: It is the kind of intermediary worker that the consumer contacts most frequently. An open or forward proxy server is a type of intermediary that accepts requests from web clients and then browses websites to get the requested information. It sends the information straight to internet users after gathering the information from the websites. It gets over the government-made barrier. Forward proxy setup is displayed inside the image below.

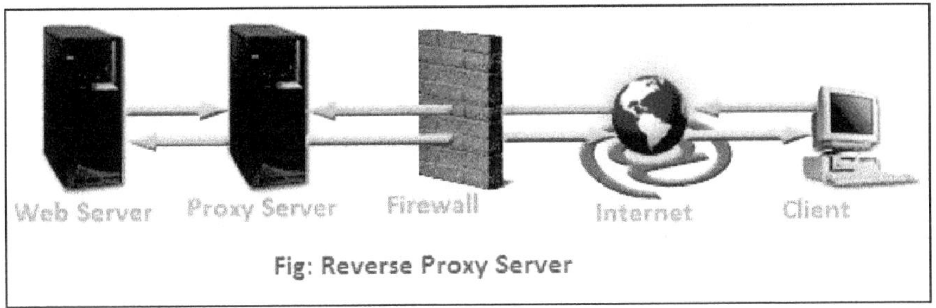

Fig: Reverse Proxy Server

1. **Split Proxy Server:** It is implemented as two programs installed on two different computers.
2. **Transparent Proxy:** It is a proxy server that does not modify the request or response beyond what is required for proxy authentication and identification. It works on port 80.
3. **Non-Transparent Proxy:** It is an intermediary that alters the solicitation reaction to offer some extra types of assistance to the client. Web demands are straightforwardly shipped off the intermediary paying little mind to the worker from where they started.
4. **Hostile Proxy:** It is used to eavesdrop upon the data flow between the client machine and the web.
5. **Intercepting Proxy Server:** It combines the proxy server with a gateway. It is commonly used in businesses to prevent avoidance of acceptable use policy and ease of administration.
6. **Forced Proxy Server:** It is a combination of Intercepting and non-intercepting policies.
7. **Caching Proxy Server:** Caching is servicing the request of clients with the help of saved contents from previous requests, without communicating with the specified server.
8. **Web Proxy Server:** The proxy that is targeted to the world wide web is known as a web proxy server.
9. **Anonymous Proxy:** The server tries to anonymizing the web surfing.
10. **Socks Proxy:** It is an ITEF (Internet Engineering Task Force) standard. It is just like a proxy system that supports proxy-aware applications. It does not allow the external network components to collects the information of the client that had generated the request. It consists of the following

components:

1. A dient library for the SOCK.
2. A dient program such as FTP, telnet, or internet browser.
3. A SOCK server for the specified operating system.

11. **High Anonymity Proxy:** The proxy server that doesn't contain the proxy server type and the client IP address in a request header. Clients using the proxy can't be tracked.
12. **Rotating Proxy:** It assigns a unique IP address to each client who is connected to it. It is ideal for users who do a lot of continuous web scrapping. It allows us to return the same website again and again. So, using the rotating proxy requires more attention.
13. **SSL Proxy Server:** It decrypts the data between the client and the server. It means data is encrypted in both directions. Since proxy hides its existence from both the client and the server. It is best suited for organizations that enhance protection against threats. In SSL proxy, the content encrypted is not cached.
14. **Shared Proxy:** The consumer is reached via the most well-known category of intermediary worker. The phrase "open or forward proxy server" refers to the several categories of intermediaries that accept requests from web clients and then browse websites to get the requested information. The information is directly forwarded to internet users after being collected from the websites. The government-built barrier is disregarded. The setup for a forward proxy is shown in the figure below.
15. **Public Proxy:** The consumer may reach this sort of intermediate worker the most frequently. An open or forward proxy server is a type of intermediary that accepts requests from web clients and then browses locations to get the requested information. It sends the data straight to internet users after gathering it from the websites. It gets over the government-built barrier. The configuration of a forward proxy is shown in the picture below.
16. **Residential Proxy:** It is the kind of intermediary worker that the consumer contacts most frequently. An open or forward proxy server is a type of intermediary that accepts requests from web clients and then browses websites to get the requested information. It sends the information straight to internet users after gathering the information from the websites. It gets over the government-made barrier. Forward

proxy setup is displayed in the image below.

17. **Distorting Proxy:** It is different from others because it identifies itself as a proxy to a website but hides its own identity. The actual IP address is changed by providing an incorrect one. It is perfect for clients who do not want to disclose their location during surfing.
18. **Data Center Proxy:** It is a special type of proxy that is not affiliated with the ISP. It is provided by other corporations through a data center. These servers can be found in physical data centers. It is ideal for clients who want quick responses. It does not provide high-level anonymity. For this reason, it can put client information at high risk.
19. **HTTP Proxy:**HTTP proxies are those proxy servers that are used to save cache files of the browsed websites. It saves time and enhances the speed because cached files reside in the local memory. If the user again wants to access the same file proxy itself provides the same file without actually browsing the pages.

Advantages of Proxy Server: There are the following benefits of using the proxy server:

- It improves the security and enhances the privacy of the user.
- It hides the identity (IP address) of the user.
- It controls the traffic and prevents crashes.
- Also, saves bandwidth by caching files and compressing incoming traffic.
- Protect our network from malware.
- Allows access to the restricted content.

Need of Proxy Server

- It reduces the chances of data breaches.
- It adds a subsidiary layer of security between server and outside traffic.
- It also protects from hackers.
- It filters the requests.

Working of Proxy Server:

The consumer is able to reach this sort of intermediary worker the most frequently. Any type of intermediary that accepts requests from web clients and then browses locations to acquire the requested information is referred to as an open or forward proxy server. It transmits the data straight to internet users after gathering it from the websites. It avoids the government-built barrier. The setup of a forward proxy is illustrated in the figure below.

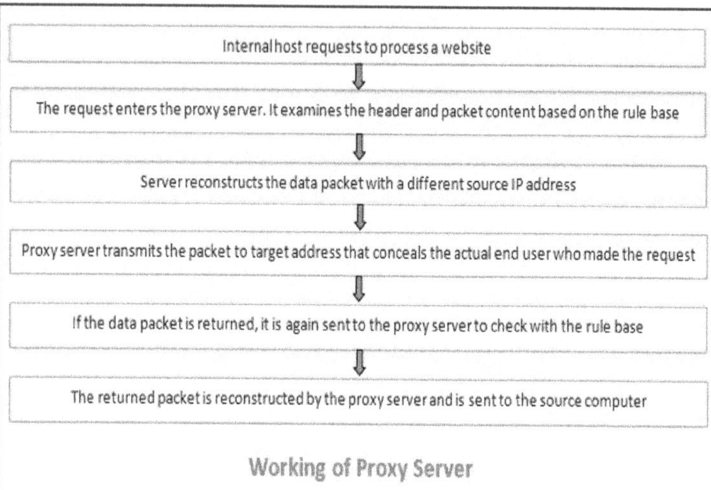

Working of Proxy Server

Overall, it can be said that the proxy server accesses the targeted site, on behalf of the client, and collects all the requested information, and forwards them to the user (client). The following figure clearly depicts the working of the proxy server.

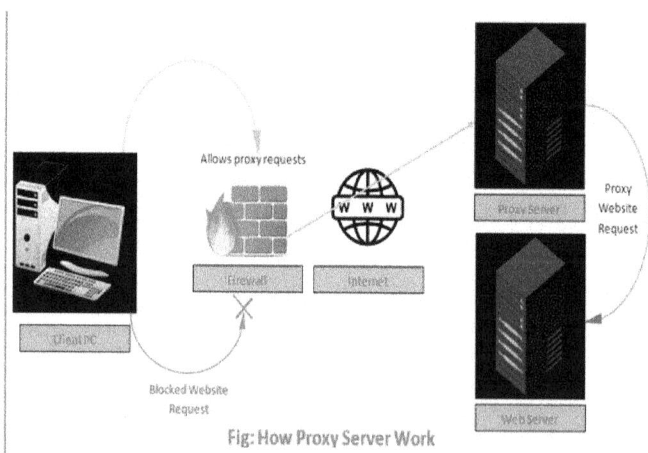

Fig: How Proxy Server Work

VPN vs. Proxy Server: Virtual Private Networks (VPNs) and proxy servers both provide comparable functions. Both provide users the option to conceal their IP addresses, locations, and access to blocked websites. The main distinction is that a VPN encrypts all communication, whereas a proxy server does not. Another distinction is that while proxy server users' activities may be monitored, VPN users' activities cannot be monitored.

Basis of Comparison	**Proxy Server**	**VPN**
Encryption	It does not encrypt the traffic.	It encrypts the traffic.
Software	It does not have its own software.	It has its own software.
Speed	It is faster than VPN.	It is slower in comparison to the proxy server.
Cache	It uses cache.	It does not use cache.
IP Address	It hides the IP address but the proxy owner can see the client's IP address.	The IP address is completely hidden.
Connection	It is unstable.	It is seamless.
Pricing	It is mostly free.	It is chargeable.
Reliability	Its connection drops more frequently.	Its connection is more reliable.
Level of Working	It works on the application level.	It works on the operating system level.
Security	It is less secure.	It provides greater security.

CHAPTER FIVE

IP ADDRESSING SCHEMA

What is address space?

The amount of memory allotted for all potential addresses for a computational object, such as a device, file, server, or networked computer, is known as address space. Each device and process is given address space by the system, which contains a certain chunk of the processor's address space. This can comprise processor-accessible physical or virtual addresses as well as addresses set aside for certain processes.

The processor's address space is frequently constrained by the width of its address bus and registers. However, a memory management method known as virtual memory can expand the address space such that it is larger than the actual memory.

Virtual vs. physical memory

VIRTUAL RAM	RAM
Uses a segment of physical memory	Physical memory
Slower	Faster
Uses paging	Uses swapping techniques
Limited by the size of the physical memory	Limited to the size of the RAM chip
Does not have direct access to the CPU	Can directly access the CPU
Limited by the size of the computer's hard drive	Can add RAM by installing more RAM chips

There are two types of address space: flat and segmented. Integers starting at zero and growing progressively are used to depict flat address spaces. Independent segments augmented by offsets or values added to create secondary addresses represent segmented addresses.

In some systems, address space can be converted from one format to another through a thunking process -- low-level, machine-generated code used to deploy details of a software system. Thunking is often used to delay calculations until the system requires a result.

Some types of address spaces

Here are a few examples of address spaces.

Virtual address space: A virtual address is a binary number in the virtual memory that enables applications to access a particular location in main storage. This allows use of the primary memory to go unhindered by other processes and facilitates the use of additional storage beyond that which is really available. Relegating certain material to a hard drive or internal flash memory is how it functions.

A logical address space is a collection of logical addresses that a computer creates for a particular software. A physical address space is a collection of physical addresses that are mapped to equivalent logical addresses.

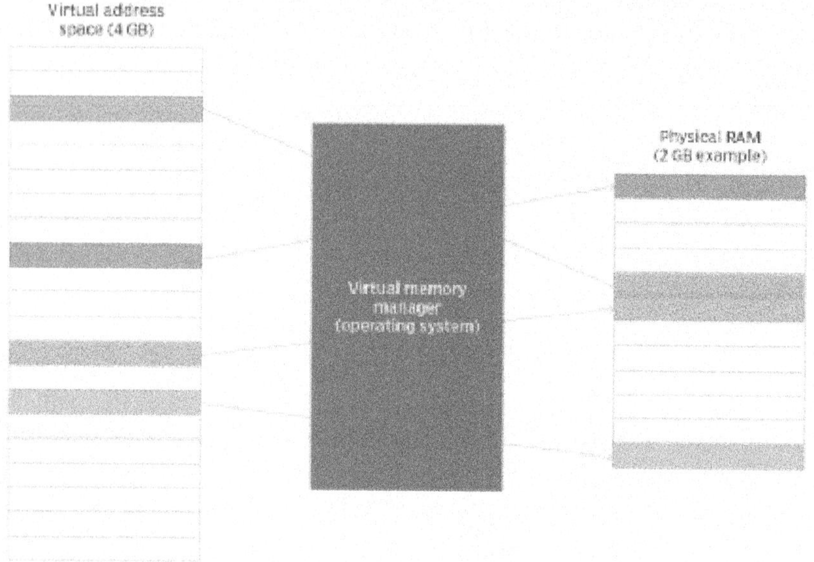

This diagram illustrates process of assigning addresses to virtual and physical memory (RAM).

IPv4 to IPv6

In terms of IP address space, concern emerged that the 32-bit address space of IP version 4 (IPv4) would be inadequate to support the enormous growth of the internet. So, IPv6 was developed with its 128-bit address space.

Subnetting IPv6 address space

By subnetting a portion of a network address space, the main goal of subnetting IPv6 address space is to increase the efficiency of address allocation. Reducing traffic on a large network by dividing it into smaller, linked groups of networks boosts network performance by preventing data from taking extraneous paths. The host address range and network component of the IP address are shared by the computer and the subnet mask, respectively. The host address range consists of the addresses given to network hosts.

Subnet segmentation illustrated

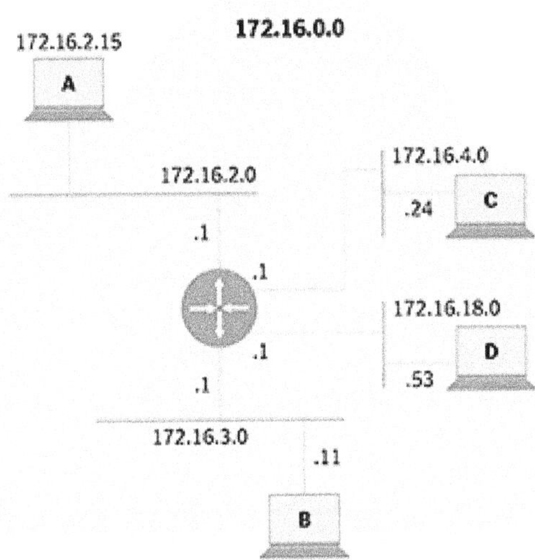

Subnetting improves the efficiency of address allocation, splitting a larger network into smaller groups of interconnected networks.

Address space layout randomization

Address space layout randomization is a memory security mechanism used to prevent potential exploitation of memory corruption vulnerabilities. Adding randomness into a process's virtual memory address space makes it challenging to exploit vulnerabilities.

Address space in Microsoft Azure

In Microsoft Azure, a virtual network's address space consists of one or more non-overlapping addresses. These address ranges are defined in classless inter-domain routing notations, along with their public or private status. The custom private IP address space is supplied when building a virtual network utilising both public and private addresses. From the address space you choose in a virtual network, Azure then allots resources, including a private IP address.

Address space vs. memory space

The addresses programmers use are called virtual addresses. A set of these virtual addresses is called address space.

The place where the address was saved in the main memory is known as the location. A group of locations is called memory space.

Address space translation

Address space translation describes the process of concentrating the frame number with the offset part of a logical address. This approach helps form a physical address.

class full addressing : IP address is an address having information about how to reach a specific host, especially outside the LAN. An IP address is a 32 bit unique address having an address space of 2^{32}.

Generally, there are two notations in which IP address is written, dotted decimal notation and hexadecimal notation.

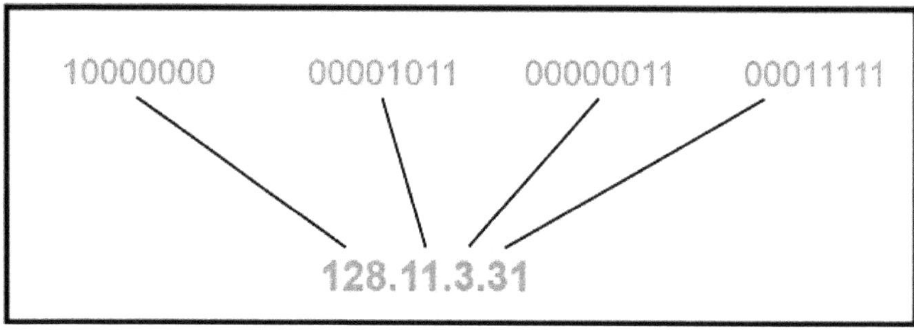

Dotted Decimal Notation

01110101	00011101	10010101	11101010
75	1D	95	EA

0x751D95EA

Hexadecimal Notation

Some points to be noted about dotted decimal notation:

1. The value of any segment (byte) is between 0 and 255 (both included).
2. There are no zeroes preceding the value in any segment (054 is wrong, 54 is correct).

Classful Addressing: The 32 bit IP address is divided into five sub-classes. These are:

- Class A
- Class B
- Class C
- Class D
- Class E

There is a suitable range of IP addresses for each of these classes. For multicast and experimental reasons, respectively, classes D and E are set aside. The order of bits in the first octet determine the classes of IP address. IPv4 address is divided into two parts:

- Network ID
- Host ID

The bits used for network ID and host ID as well as the maximum number of networks and hosts that can be included in a given class of IP address are determined by the class. Each device connected to a network is given an IP address by the ISP or network administrator in charge of that network.

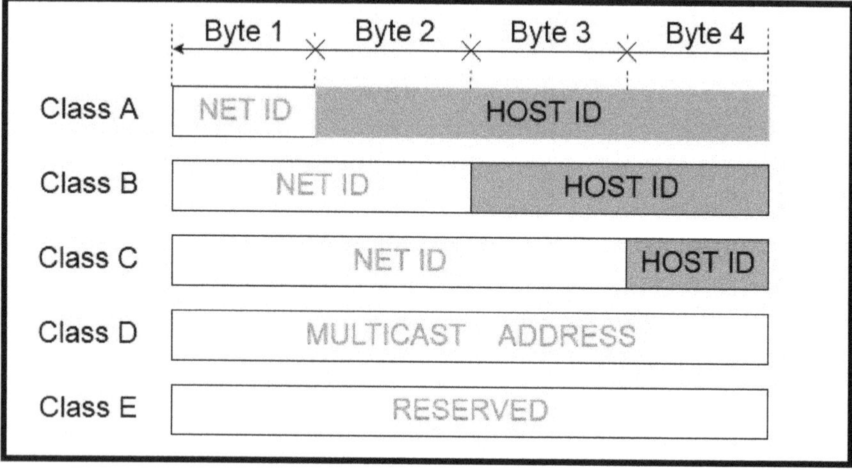

Note: IP addresses are globally managed by Internet Assigned Numbers Authority(IANA) and regional Internet registries(RIR).

Note: While finding the total number of host IP addresses, 2 IP addresses are not counted and are therefore, decreased from the total count because the first IP address of any network is the network number and whereas the last IP address is reserved for broadcast IP.

Class A:

IP address belonging to class A are assigned to the networks that contain a large number of hosts.

- The network ID is 8 bits long.
- The host ID is 24 bits long.

The higher order bit of the first octet in class A is always set to 0. The remaining 7 bits in first octet are used to determine network ID. The 24 bits of host ID are used to determine the host in any network. The default subnet mask for class A is 255.x.x.x. Therefore, class A has a total of:

- 2^7-2= 126 network ID(Here 2 address is subtracted because 0.0.0.0 and 127.x.y.z are special address.)
- 2^24 – 2 = 16,777,214 host ID

IP addresses belonging to class A ranges from 1.x.x.x – 126.x.x.x

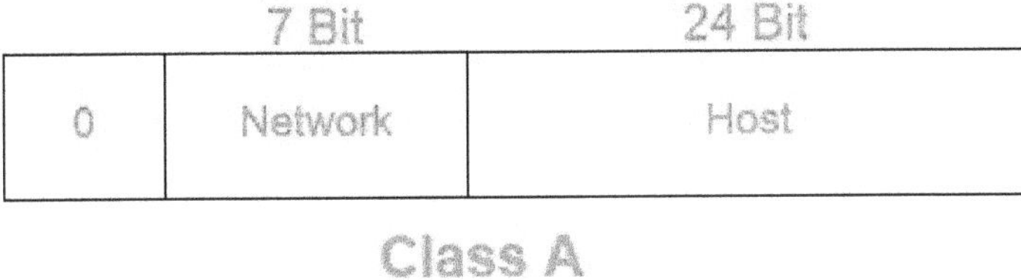

Class B: IP address belonging to class B are assigned to the networks that ranges from medium-sized to large-sized networks.

- The network ID is 16 bits long.
- The host ID is 16 bits long.

The higher order bits of the first octet of IP addresses of class B are always set to 10. The remaining 14 bits are used to determine network ID. The 16 bits of host ID is used to determine the host in any network. The default sub-net mask for class B is 255.255.x.x. Class B has a total of:

- 2^14 = 16384 network address
- 2^16 – 2 = 65534 host address

IP addresses belonging to class B ranges from 128.0.x.x – 191.255.x.x.

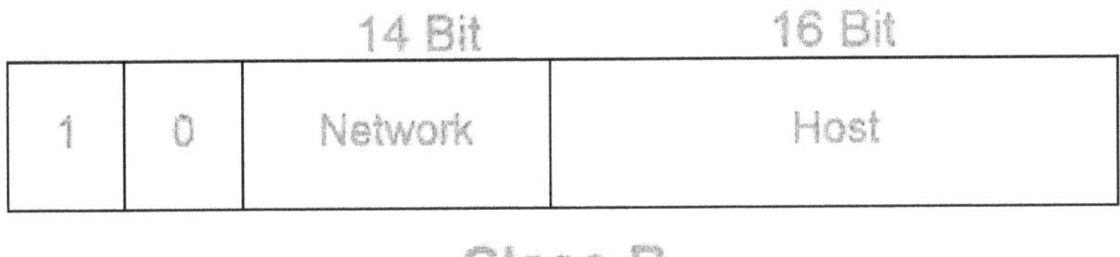

Class C: IP address belonging to class C are assigned to small-sized networks.

- The network ID is 24 bits long.

- The host ID is 8 bits long.

The higher order bits of the first octet of IP addresses of class C are always set to 110. The remaining 21 bits are used to determine network ID. The 8 bits of host ID is used to determine the host in any network. The default sub-net mask for class C is 255.255.255.x. Class C has a total of:

- 2^21 = 2097152 network address
- 2^8 – 2 = 254 host address

IP addresses belonging to class C ranges from 192.0.0.x – 223.255.255.x.

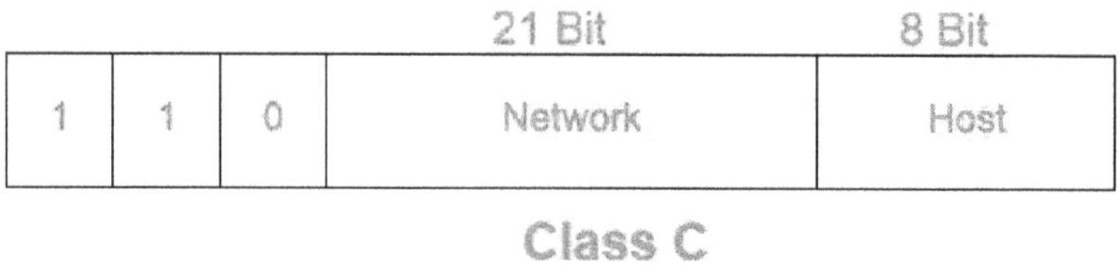

			21 Bit	8 Bit
1	1	0	Network	Host

Class C

Class D: IP address belonging to class D are reserved for multi-casting. The higher order bits of the first octet of IP addresses belonging to class D are always set to 1110. The remaining bits are for the address that interested hosts recognize. Class D does not posses any sub-net mask. IP addresses belonging to class D ranges from 224.0.0.0 – 239.255.255.255.

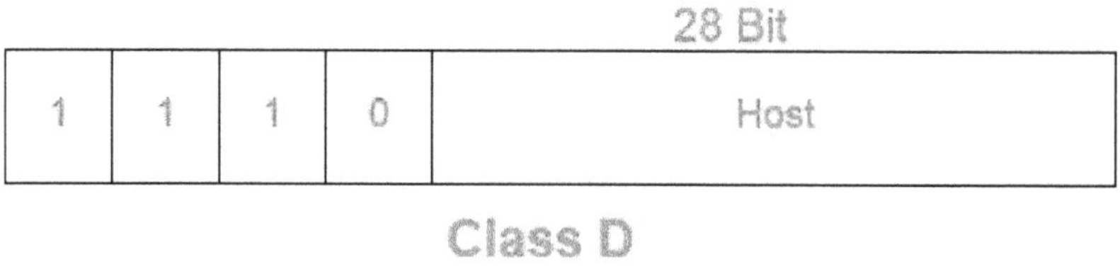

				28 Bit
1	1	1	0	Host

Class D

Class E: IP addresses belonging to class E are reserved for experimental and research purposes. IP addresses of class E ranges from 240.0.0.0 – 255.255.255.254. This class doesn't have any sub-net mask. The higher order bits of first octet of class E are always set to 1111.

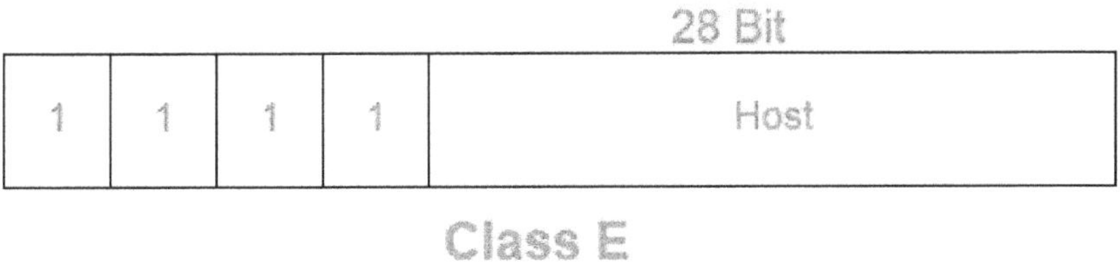

28 Bit

1	1	1	1	Host

Class E

Range of special IP addresses:

169.254.0.0 – 169.254.0.16 : Link local addresses

127.0.0.0 – 127.0.0.8 : Loop-back addresses

0.0.0.0 – 0.0.0.8 : used to communicate within the current network.

Rules for assigning Host ID: Host ID's are used to identify a host within a network. The host ID are assigned based on the following rules:

- Within any network, the host ID must be unique to that network.
- Host ID in which all bits are set to 0 cannot be assigned because this host ID is used to represent the network ID of the IP address.
- Host ID in which all bits are set to 1 cannot be assigned because this host ID is reserved as a broadcast address to send packets to all the hosts present on that particular network.

Rules for assigning Network ID: Hosts that are located on the same physical network are identified by the network ID, as all host on the same physical network is assigned the same network ID. The network ID is assigned based on the following rules:

- The network ID cannot start with 127 because 127 belongs to class A address and is reserved for internal loop-back functions.
- All bits of network ID set to 1 are reserved for use as an IP broadcast address and therefore, cannot be used.
- All bits of network ID set to 0 are used to denote a specific host on the local network and are not routed and therefore, aren't used.

CLASS	LEADING BITS	NET ID BITS	HOST ID BITS	NO. OF NETWORKS	ADDRESSES PER NETWORK	START ADDRESS	END ADDRESS
CLASS A	0	8	24	2^7 (128)	2^{24} (16,777,216)	0.0.0.0	127.255.255.255
CLASS B	10	16	16	2^{14} (16,384)	2^{16} (65,536)	128.0.0.0	191.255.255.255
CLASS C	110	24	8	2^{21} (2,097,152)	2^8 (256)	192.0.0.0	223.255.255.255
CLASS D	1110	NOT DEFINED	NOT DEFINED	NOT DEFINED	NOT DEFINED	224.0.0.0	239.255.255.255
CLASS E	1111	NOT DEFINED	NOT DEFINED	NOT DEFINED	NOT DEFINED	240.0.0.0	255.255.255.255

Summary of Classful addressing

The issue with this classful addressing system is that millions of class A addresses are thrown away, along with numerous class B addresses and a dearth of class C addresses that are insufficient to meet the demands of companies. Class D addresses are only accessible in one block since they are utilised for multicast routing. Addresses in the class E are reserved.

Network Address and Mask: Network address – It identifies a network on internet. Using this, we can find range of addresses in the network and total possible number of hosts in the network.

Mask – It is a 32-bit binary number that gives the network address in the address block when AND operation is bitwise applied on the mask and any IP address of the block.

The default mask in different classes are :

Class A – 255.0.0.0

Class B – 255.255.0.0

Class C – 255.255.255.0

Example : Given IP address 132.6.17.85 and default class B mask, find the beginning address (network address).

Solution : The default mask is 255.255.0.0, which means that the only the first 2 bytes are preserved and the other 2 bytes are set to 0. Therefore, the network address is 132.6.0.0.

Subnetting: Subnetting is the process of breaking up a big block of addresses into several contiguous subblocks and allocating these subblocks to various smaller networks. When classless addressing is utilised, this procedure is common.

Classless Addressing: Sub-netting is used to reduce the waste of IP addresses inside a block. We utilise the host id bits of a classful IP address as the net id bits. We specify the IP address and the number of mask bits along with it (often denoted by the sign "/"); for example, 192.168.1.1/28. In this case, the subnet mask is determined by setting the specified number of bits out of 32 to 1. For example, in the provided address, we must set 28 of the 32 bits to 1 and the remaining 16 to 0. As a result, the subnet mask is 255.255.255.240.

Some values calculated in subnetting :

1. Number of subnets : Given bits for mask – No. of bits in default mask
2. Subnet address : AND result of subnet mask and the given IP address
3. Broadcast address : By putting the host bits as 1 and retaining the network bits as in the IP address
4. Number of hosts per subnet : $2^{(32 - \text{Given bits for mask})} - 2$
5. First Host ID : Subnet address + 1 (adding one to the binary representation of the subnet address)
6. Last Host ID : Subnet address + Number of Hosts

Example : Given IP Address – 172.16.0.0/25, find the number of subnets and the number of hosts per subnet. Also, for the first subnet block, find the subnet address, first host ID, last host ID and broadcast address.

Solution : This is a class B address. So, no. of subnets = $2^{(25-16)} = 2^9 = 512$.

No. of hosts per subnet = $2^{(32-25)} - 2 = 2^7 - 2 = 128 - 2 = 126$

For the first subnet block, we have subnet address = 0.0, first host id = 0.1, last host id = 0.126 and broadcast address = 0.127

Protocol Analyzers (Wireshark): Protocol Analyzers A set of guidelines known as the network protocol governs data transmission and communication through networks and the internet. To communicate and share data, both the transmitter and receiver must adhere to the same protocols. Whenever we access a website or exchange some data with another device, then these processes are governed by a set of rules called the internet protocols.

Working: Data is arranged into tiny units called packets, which is how the internet and many other data networks operate. The underlying technology and software divide each huge data into little packets, which are subsequently delivered between two network devices. The packets are put back together into the original when they reach their destination. Each network protocol defines the rules for how its data packets must be organized in a specific way according to the protocols the network supports.

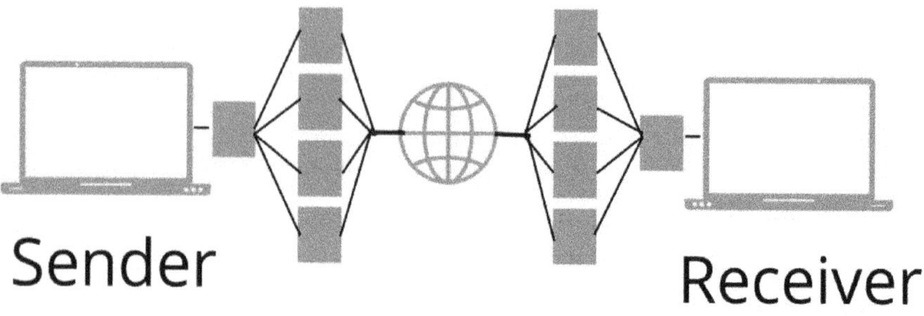

Protocol Analyzer: A tool that enables you to track and examine network traffic is a protocol analyzer. It may be used for network performance monitoring, security issue detection, and troubleshooting. The fundamental goal of protocol analyzers is to assist us in comprehending the manner in which packets are sent across a network. It is a piece of hardware or software that is used to gather and examine data from a channel of communication between two or more devices. Its main function is to capture digital data on the communication channel that two or more devices use to communicate with each other and convert the digital data bits into an information protocol sequence. Satellite connections and local computer buses are two examples of communication channels.

Type of Protocol Analyzer: As mentioned above, a protocol analyzer is a hardware or software tool. Therefore, there are two kinds of protocol analyzers in the industry.

- **Hardware Protocol Analyzer:** As the name suggests, it is a hardware-based protocol analyzer that uses both hardware and software to capture and analyze the packets transmitted by the interface for downstream analysis. Some hardware-based protocol analyzers are the UFS protocol analyzer and eMMC protocol analyzer, PCIe protocol analyzer, and many more.
- **Software Protocol Analyzer:** As the name propose, it is a software-based protocol analyzer that uses only software to collect and analyze the protocol. A software protocol analyzer is also known as a network analyzer because it is used to collect and analyze local area networks, wireless networks, etc.

Uses: The following points explain why the protocol analyzer is useful:

- With the protocol analyzer, the development time can be greatly shortened.
- Capturing and analyzing the protocol transferred packet of data and analysis of complex protocol is going to be easier with a protocol analyzer.
- With protocol analyzer inbuilt software, the error in detection is greatly reduced to zero.
- Many protocol analyzers now have API integration to create fully automated test cases that can be used to easily create complex test cases to validate systems.
- The protocol analyzer provides quick notification or reports when there is any violation in the protocol and ensures that the protocol standard complies.
- With the protocol analyzer, bus faults in embedded systems can be easily reported.

Wireshark: Wireshark is a software tool used to monitor the network traffic through a network interface. It is the most widely used network monitoring tool today. Wireshark is loved equally by system administrators, network engineers, network enthusiasts, network security professionals and black hat hackers.

The extent of its popularity is such, that experience with Wireshark is considered as a valuable/essential trait in a computer networking-related professional.

There are many reasons why Wireshark is so popular :

1. It has a great GUI as well as a conventional CLI(T Shark).
2. It offers network monitoring on almost all types of network standards (ethernet, wlan, Bluetooth etc)
3. It is open-source with a large community of backers and developers.
4. All the necessary components for monitoring, analyzing and documenting the network traffic are present. It is free to use.

History of Wireshark: With the goal of creating a tool for in-depth network packet analysis, Wireshark was founded. Gerald Combez founded it in 1997. Its initial name was Ethereal. It was initially released in July 1998 as version 0.2.0. Due to the support it got from the developer community, it grew rapidly and was released as version 1.0 in 2008, almost two years after it was renamed to Wireshark.

Wireshark installation:

Windows :

- You can do a proper installation or run Wireshark as a portable app on your windows system. To download tNormalhe installation executable or the portable app go to Wireshark Downloads
- Run the executable and follow on-screen instructions to complete the installation.

On Linux:

- Install using your package manager. See the manual for your package manager for correct syntax.
  Most Debian Linux OS have apt(advanced packaging tool) package manager pre-installed. Similarly Fedora family of OS have "yum" package manager pre-installed.
  The generic command is

- html

<package-manager-name> install Wireshark

Wireshark installation in ubuntu/ Linux :

Open terminal in your system or press ALT + CTRL + T and run the below command:

sudo add-apt-repository ppa:wireshark-dev/stable

Update the repository:

sudo apt-get update

Install wire shark using thebelow command:

sudo apt-get install wireshark

To run the wire shark use thebelow command

sudo wireshark

You can opt for a security-based Linux OS that has Wireshark pre-installed, like Kali Linux.

The basic features of Wireshark are:

Packet Monitor: This segment visually shows the packets flowing inside the network. There are color codes for each type of packet. The packets are shown with the following information :

1. Source address
2. Destination address
3. Packet type
4. Hex dump of the packet
5. Contents of the packet in text
6. Source port(if applicable)
7. Destination port(if applicable)

Import from a capture file: This feature lets you import packets dump from a capture file to analyse further. There are many formats supported by Wireshark, some of them are:

- pcapng
- libpcap
- Oracle snoop and atmsnoop
- Finisar (previously Shomiti) Surveyor captures
- Microsoft Network Monitor captures
- Novell LANalyzer captures
- AIX iptrace captures
- Cinco Networks NetXray captures
- Network Associates Windows-based Sniffer and Sniffer Pro captures
- Network General/Network Associates DOS-based Sniffer (compressed or uncompressed) captures
- AG Group/WildPackets/Savvius EtherPeek/TokenPeek/AiroPeek/EtherHelp/PacketGrabber captures
- RADCOM's WAN/LAN Analyzer captures
- Network Instruments Observer version 9 captures
- Lucent/Ascend router debug output
- HP-UX's nettl
- Toshiba's ISDN routers dump output
- ISDN4BSD i4btrace utility
- Traces from the EyeSDN USB S0
- IPLog format from the Cisco Secure Intrusion Detection System
- the output from VMS's TCPIPtrace/TCPtrace/UCX$TRACE utilities

- the text output from the DBS Etherwatch VMS utility
- Visual Networks' Visual UpTime traffic capture
- the output from CoSine L2 debug
- the output from Accellent's 5Views LAN agents
- Endace Measurement Systems' ERF format captures
- Linux Bluez Bluetooth stack hcidump -w traces
- Catapult DCT2000 .out files
- Gammu generated text output from Nokia DCT3 phones in Netmonitor mode
- IBM Series (OS/400) Comm traces (ASCII & UNICODE)
- Juniper Netscreen snoop captures
- Symbian OS btsnoop captures
- Tamosoft CommView captures
- Textronix K12xx 32bit .rf5 format captures
- Textronix K12 text file format captures
- Apple PacketLogger captures
- Captures from Aethra Telecommunications' PC108 software

Export to a capture file: Wireshark lets you save the results as a capture file to continue working on them at later point of time. The supported formats are:

- pcapng (*.pcapng)
- libpcap, tcpdump and various other tools using tcpdump's capture format (*.pcap, *.cap, *.dmp)
- Accellent 5Views (*.5vw)
- HP-UX's nettl (*.TRC0, *.TRC1)
- Microsoft Network Monitor – NetMon (*.cap)
- Network Associates Sniffer – DOS (*.cap, *.enc, *.trc, *fdc, *.syc)
- Network Associates Sniffer – Windows (*.cap)
- Network Instruments Observer version 9 (*.bfr)
- Novell LANalyzer (*.tr1)
- Oracle (previously Sun) snoop (*.snoop, *.cap)
- Visual Networks Visual UpTime traffic (*.*).

As a novice, you should concentrate mainly on being familiar with the fundamentals of the Wireshark UI and other fundamentals (the formats provided here are only for your perusal; you are under no need to use them at this time).

After completing these foundational steps, you may begin experimenting with the tool. Open Wireshark, choose an interface—make sure it's talking right now—you can tell by the zigzag pattern in front of the interface name—and click the fin icon to begin catching packets. Once you're done seeing the traffic, save the outcome as a capture file and close the programme. This concludes the fundamentals.

Short Questions With Answers

1. ___ network used for communication between the computer and different information technological devices close to one person.

Ans. PAN

2. A ___ often uses transmission facilities provided by common carriers, such as telephone companies.

Ans. WAN

3. A ___ is a network topology consisting of a main run of cable with a terminator at each end.

Ans. linear bus topology

4. What will be the total number of links in a mesh network topology if n nodes are connected to each other?

Ans. n (n-1)

5. How are ISO and OSI related to each other?

Ans. The Open Systems Interconnection (OSI) reference model was defined by the International Standards Organization (ISO) as the first step towards international standardization.

6. OSI stands for ___.

Ans. Open Systems Interconnection

7. Application layer of the OSI model is concerned with the syntax and semantics of the information transfer between two systems. (True/False).

Ans. Physical address

8. ___ address encodes the manufacturer's registered identification number and may be mentioned to as the burned-in address.

Ans. False: Since the presentation, the layer is concerned with the syntax and semantics of the information transfer between two systems.

9. Choose the correct option?

Which layer incorporates the physical address in a frame?

a) Physical layer

b) Data link layer

c) Network layer

d) Presentation layer

Ans. b) Data link layer

10. What is the size Ethernet physical address?

Ans. 6 byte or 48 bit

11. ___ is nothing but a connector, which connect multiple wires coming from different branches.

Ans. Passive hub

12. Bridge is a three-layer switch that use the logical address to transmit the packet to a destination. (true/false).

Ans. False: Since the router is a three-layer switch use the logical address to transmit a packet to the proper destination.

13. What is multiplexing?

Ans. Multiplexing is a method by which the whole capacity of a connected link can be shared by multiple users for better productivity.

14. In ___ the data flow of each input connection is divided into units and time into some fixed slots.

Ans. synchronous TDM

15. How WDM differ from FDM?

Ans. Conceptually they are similar, only thing is WDM is purposefully designed for fibre-optic cable to support high data-rate.

16. Ethernet uses the ___ protocol for resolution of multiple accesses to the broadcast channel in the MAC sub-layer-before data transmission begins.

Ans. CSMA/CD

17. Match the followings:

Set 1 Set II

1) 100BASE-TX A) Fibre optic cables

2) 100BASE-T4 B) Two pairs of high-quality twisted-pair wires

3) 100BASE-FX C) four pairs of normal quality twisted pair wires

a) 1. A, 2. B, 3. C

b) 1. A, 2. C, 3. B

c) 1. C, 2. A, 3. B

d) 1. B, 2. C, 3. A

Ans. d) 1. B, 2. C, 3. A

18. Token Ring is a LAN with ___ or ___ throughput.

Ans. 4 or 16 Mbits/s

19. FDDI stands for ___.

Ans. Fibre distributed data interface

20. Token ring local area network (LAN) technology is a local area network protocol that resides at the ___ of the OSI model.

a) physical layer b) data link layer

c) network layer d) session layer

Ans. b) data link layer

21. What are the three important phases of circuit switching?

Ans. Three important phases of circuit switching are connection establishment, data transfer and connection disconnect.

22. In the ___ approach each packet with the same destination need not follow the same route to reach the destination.

Ans. datagram

23. VCI stands for ___.

Ans. virtual circuit identifier

24. What type of switching is also known as store-and-forward switching?

Ans. message switching

25. SONET/SDH is channelized (True/False)

Ans. True

26. What is the data rate of the SONET STS-1 frame?

Ans. 51.84 Mbps

27. The SONET STS-3 frame consists of ___ bytes and is transmitted 8000 times per second.

Ans. 2430

28. SONET/SDH rings are interconnected to cover a wide geographical area via ___.

Ans. digital cross-connect systems

29. What SONET device receives an OC-N signal from which it can demultiplex and terminate any number of DSn and/or OC-M signals? When M < N?

Ans. SONET/SDH add/drop multiplexer

30. DWDM stands for ___.

Ans. Dense wavelength division multiplexing

31. What is an optical supervisory channel?

Ans. The optical supervisory channel is an additional wavelength usually outside the EDFA amplification band. It carries information about the multi-wavelength optical signal as well as remote conditions at the optical terminal or EDFA site.

32. These carrier frequencies are separated by adequate bandwidth to accommodate the modulated signal is called.

Ans. channel

33. SONET network is one of the applications of ___.

Ans. WDM

34. At the time SONET was devised, the highest-speed digital carrier actually used widely in the United States was T3, at ___.

Ans. 44.736 Mbps

35. ___ is ISDN – compatible equipment, that is, equipment that can interface directly to an ISDN circuit via a four-wire twisted – pair interfaces.

Ans. TE1

36. Choose the correct option:

a) Terminal Adapters (TAs), also known as ISDN ___, are interface adapters for connecting one or more TE2 (non – ISDN) devices to an ISDN network.

b) reference point

c) modems

d) transmitter

e) adapter

Ans. modems

37. Basic rate interfaces provide the user with two ___ channels for data transmission (B channels) and one ___ channel for the transmission of signalling information (a D channel).

Ans. 64 Kbps, 16 Kbps

38. Choose the correct option:

___ provide users with the possibility of high-speed data transmission at rates of 384 Kbps, 1,536 Kbps or 1,920 Kbps.

a) B channels

b) C channels

c) D channels

d) H channels

Ans. H channels

39. The ISDN ___ supports signalling and control messages between user TE and the carrier networks, both circuit-switched and packet-switched, and between TE devices in a user – to – user private network.

Ans. D channel

40. In the LAP-D frame format the flag field is a two-octet field that delimits (i.e., establishes the limits or boundaries of) the beginning and end of the frame. (True/False)

Ans. False: Since, in LAP-D frame format the flag field is a one – octet field that delimits (i.e., establishes the limits or boundaries of) the beginning and end of the frame.

41. B – ISDN user access is ___ in nature, relying on SDH/SONET fibre – optic transmission standards.

Ans. broadband

42. In B-ISDN ___ involve the bidirectional transmission and include three classes of service.

Ans. Interactive services

43. Choose the correct option:

In ___ systems, clocks run close to each other, within a well-defined tolerance.

a) Asynchronous

b) Synchronous

c) plesiochronous

d) Omni synchronous

Ans. c) plesiochronous

44. The ___ carrier system is used in North America to carry the DS signal, and the ___ carrier system is used to carry the international digital hierarchy.

Ans. T, E

45. SONET stands for ___.

Ans. Synchronous Optical Network

46. Contemporary computer systems communicate in ___ mode through variations in electrical voltage.

Ans. Binary/digital

47. What is the traffic measurement unit in case of the analogue network?

Ans. Hz

48. In the case of digital network power requirement is high. (True/ False)

Ans. False: Since in the case of digital network power requirement is low.

49. ISDN stands for ___.

Ans. Integrated Service Digital Network

50. The process of setting a virtual path connection is decoupled from the process of setting up an individual virtual channel connection (True/ False)

Ans. True

51. Frame Relay is an example of ___ protocol.

Ans. packet switching

52. ATM does the data transfer in the form of ___.

Ans. Desecrate chunks

53. A switched connection is an on-demand connection that requires call ___ for setting up and exit.

A. packets B. control signalling C. information

Ans. b) Control Signaling

54. The meta-signalling channel can also be used to set up the user-to-user signalling channel. (True/False)

Ans. True

55. The process of setting up a virtual path connection is decoupled from the process of setting up an individual virtual channel connection (True/ False).

Ans. True

56. The use of the GFC field is to control the traffic flow at the ___ ___ interface in order to improve short-term overload condition.

Ans. user-network

57. The header error control (HEC) field is carried in the final octet of the header. (True/False).

Ans. true

58. The VPI length of 8 bits allows up to ___ different virtual paths.

Ans. 256

59. The ATM cell header is composed of ___ elements.

a) 8 b) 6 c) 4 d) All the above

Ans. b) 6

60. The ABR service category is designed primarily for any type of traffic that is not ___ sensitive and expects no guarantees of service

Ans. Time

61. ATM network is designed in such a way that it supports to transfer of many different types of traffic concurrently (True/False).

Ans. True

62. NRT-VBR stands for ___

Ans. The non-real time variable bit rate

63. This layer is organized in two logical sub-layers: the ___ and ___ sub-layer.

Ans. Convergence sub-layer, segmentation-reassemble sub-layer

64. AAL 1 is designed to accommodate a constant bit rate, connection-oriented, synchronous traffic. (True/False)

Ans. True

65. The main task of AAL is ___.

Ans. Segmentation and reassembly

66. AAL2 supports a connection-oriented service in which the bit rate is variable but requires a bounded delay for delivery. (True/False)

Ans. True

67. ___ is the maximum amount of traffic that can be submitted by a source to an ATM network and is expressed as ATM cells per second.

Ans. Peak cell rate (PCR)

68. What is the maximum burst size (MBS)?

Ans. MBS is defined as the maximum number of cells that can be submitted by a source back-to-back at the peak cell rate.

69. The ___ service is the only standardized ATM service category that uses a reactive congestion control scheme.

Ans. available bit rate (ABR)

70. An X.25 network consists of switches distributed geographically and connected by high speed leased links. (True/False)

Ans. true

71. What level of X.25 protocol provides reliable transfer of data across the physical link?

Ans. data link level

72. LAP-B stands for ___.

Choose the correct option:

Ans. Link Access Protocol-Balanced

73. In X.25 network ___is a small, standalone device connected to the switch by a dedicated X.25 link.

a) Remote PAD b) Router

c) Mainframe d) None of the above

Ans. a) Remote PAD

74. In terms of the size of the network the correct order (ascending) is –

a) PAN, MAN, LAN, WAN

b) LAN, MAN, WAN, PAN

c) PAN, LAN, MAN, WAN

d) LAN, PAN, MAN, WAN

Answer: c

Explanation: Personal Area Network, Local Area Network, Metropolitan Area Network, Wide Area Network is the correct order in terms of size of the network from smallest to largest.

75. Logical Addressing and Routing are functions of which layer?

a) Physical Layer

b) Transport Layer

c) Data Link Layer

d) Network Layer

Answer: d

Explanation: . Logical Addressing and Routing are functions of the Network Layer.

76. Flow Control and Error Control are functions of which layer?

a) Physical Layer

b) Application Layer

c) Data Link Layer

d) Network Layer

Answer: c

Explanation: Flow Control and Error Control are functions of the Data Link Layer.

77. Dialog Control and Synchronization are function of which layer?

a) Presentation Layer

b) Application Layer

c) Session Layer

d) Data Link Layer

Answer: c

Explanation: Dialog Control and Synchronization are function of the Session Layer.

78. Encryption and Compression are functions of which OSI layer?

a) Presentation Layer

b) Application Layer

c) Session Layer

d) Data Link Layer

Answer: a

Explanation: Encryption and Compression are functions of the Presentation Layer.

79. How many layers are present in the TCP/IP Reference model?

a) 6

b) 7

c) 5

d) 4

Answer: d

Explanation: There are 4 layers in the TCP/IP reference model : Link, Internet, Transport and Application.

80. ______ addresses are 128 bits

Answer: IPv6

81. Which of the following TCP/IP protocols is used for transferring files form one machine to another.

A) FTP

B) SNMP

C) SMTP

D) RPC

Answer: A) FTP

82. A LAN (Local Area Network) can cover a distance of ___ KM.

A) 2

B) 8

C) 16

D) 32

Answer: A) 2

83. The types of transmission channel or media used for LAN or WAN are __.

A) Twisted Pair Cables

B) Coaxial Cables

C) Fiber-Optic Cables and Radio Waves

D) All the above

Answer: D) All the above

84. Cable TV network cables laid till your are house are __ cables.

Answer: Coaxial cables

85. Which trasmission media is easy to install inside a city to create a network quickly?

Answer: Radio Frequency devices

86. A simple WIFI modem forms a __ wireless network.

Answer: LAN

87. Which is the transmission media that can carry huge data to large distances with less delay or latency?

Answer: Optical Fiber Cables

88. Which type of network supports transmitting voice, video and data?

Answer: LAN, MAN, WAN

89. WAN or MAN may also contain __ in between to complete the network.

Answer: Leased lines, Satellite links, SMDS (Switched Multi-megabit Data Services) offered by telecom companies on point to point basis.

90. The largest WAN existing on this earth is ___.

Answer: Internet

91. The technologies used in a WAN network are __.

Answer: SONET, Frame Relay, ATM

92. A network Router works at a __ layer of an OSI reference model.

Answer: Layer 3

93. A network Bridge device connects two or more networks to form a ___ LAN network.

Answer: Single

94. The main hardware used to access a LAN resource is __.

Answer: NIU (Network Interface Unit) or NIC (Network Interface Card)

95. IEEE stands for ___.

Answer: Institute of Electrical and Electronics Engineers

96. The correct IEEE standards are used to manage various computer networks.

Answer: IEEE 802.1 = Network Management standards, IEEE 802.2 = General Data Link Layer standards, IEEE 802.3 = MAC layer protocols for a BUS network with CSMA/CD, IEEE 802.4 = MAC layer protocols for a BUS network with Token passing feature, IEEE 802.5 = MAC layer protocols for a Token RING network, IEEE 802.6 = Standards to operate a MAN (Metropolitan Area Network)

97. The cables or media used to implement 802.3 ethernet network below.

Answer: 10Base5 = Thick Coaxial cable, 10Base2 = Thin Coaxial cable, 10BaseT = Twisted Pair cable, 10BaseF = Fiber Optic cable, 10Broad36 = Broadband signalling over 75 Ohm cable

98. Who designed or invented an Ethernet network for LANs in the year 1973?

Answer: Robert Metcalfe

100. An Ethernet Jack is ___.

Answer: RJ45

Basic Practicals

Subnet a Network in Packet Tracer.

A subnet, or subnetwork, is a part of a larger network. Subnets are a logical part of an IP network into multiple, smaller network components. The Internet Protocol (IP) is the method for transmitting data from one computer to another over the internet network. Each computer, or host, on the internet, has at least one IP address as a unique identifier.

Steps to Configure and Verify Three Router Connections in Cisco Packet Tracer:

Step 1: First, open the Cisco packet tracer desktop and select the devices given below:

S.NO	Device	Model-Name	Qty.
1.	PC	pc	6
2.	Switch	PT-Switch	3
3.	Router	PT-Router	3

IP Addressing Table for PCs:

S.NO	Device	IPv4 Address	Subnet Mask	Default-Gateway
1.	pc0	192.168.1.2	255.255.255.0	192.168.1.1
2.	pc1	192.168.1.3	255.255.255.0	192.168.1.1
3.	pc2	192.168.2.2	255.255.255.0	192.168.2.1
4.	pc3	192.168.2.3	255.255.255.0	192.168.2.1
5.	pc4	192.168.3.2	255.255.255.0	192.168.3.1
6.	pc5	192.168.3.3	255.255.255.0	192.168.3.1

- Then, create a network topology as shown below the image.
- Use an Automatic connecting cable to connect the devices with others

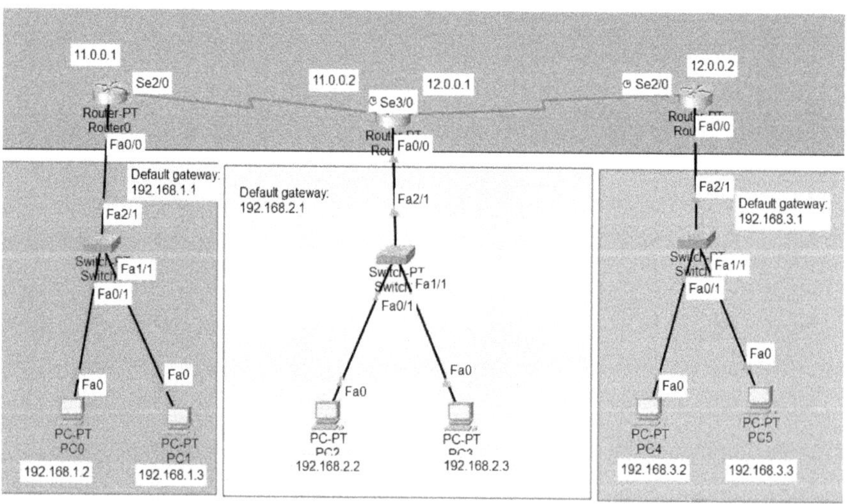

Step 2: Configure the PCs (hosts) with IPv4 address and Subnet Mask according to the IP addressing table given above.

- To assign an IP address in PC0, click on PC0.
- Then, go to desktop and then IP configuration and there you will IPv4 configuration.
- Fill IPv4 address and subnet mask.

Assigning IP address using the ipconfig command.

- Or we can also assign an IP address with the help of a command.
- Go to the command terminal of the PC.
- Example: ipconfig 192.168.1.2 255.255.255.0 192.168.1.1
-
- Then, type ipconfig <IPv4 address><subnet mask><default gateway>(if needed)

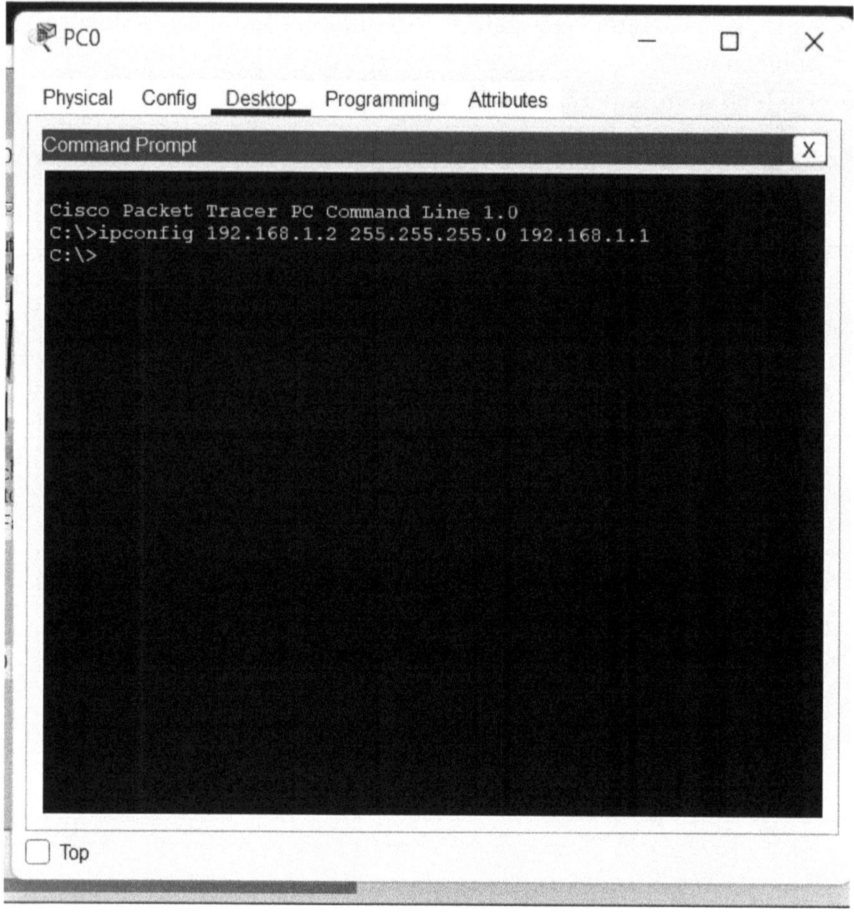

- Repeat the same procedure with other PCs to configure them thoroughly.

Step 3: Configure router with IP address and subnet mask.

IP Addressing Table Router

S.NO	Device	Interface	IPv4 Address	Subnet mask
1.	router0	FastEthernet0/0	192.168.1.1	255.255.255.0
		Serial2/0	11.0.0.1	255.0.0.0
2.	router1	Serial 2/0	11.0.0.2	255.0.0.0
		Serial 3/0	12.0.0.1	255.0.0.0
3.	router 3	FastEthernet0/0	192.168.3.1	255.255.255.0
		Serial2/0	12.0.0.2	255.0.0.0

- To assign an IP address in router0, click on router0.
- Then, go to config and then Interfaces.
- Then, configure the IP address in FastEthernet and serial ports according to IP addressing Table.
- Fill IPv4 address and subnet mask.

- Repeat the same procedure with other routers to configure them thoroughly.
- **Step 4:** After configuring all of the devices we need to assign the routes to the routers.

  To assign static routes to the particular router:
- First, click on router0 then Go to CLI.
- Then type the commands and IP information given below.
- CLI command : ip route <network id> <subnet mask><next hop>

  Static Routes for Router0 are given below:

  Router(config)#ip route 192.168.2.0 255.255.255.0 11.0.0.2

  Router(config)#ip route 11.0.0.0 255.0.0.0 11.0.0.2

  Router(config)#ip route 192.168.3.0 255.255.255.0 11.0.0.2

  Router(config)#ip route 12.0.0.0 255.0.0.0 11.0.0.2

  Static Routes for Router1 are given below:

  Router(config)#ip route 192.168.1.0 255.255.255.0 11.0.0.1

  Router(config)#ip route 11.0.0.0 255.0.0.0 11.0.0.1

Router(config)#ip route 192.168.3.0 255.255.255.0 12.0.0.2

Router(config)#ip route 12.0.0.0 255.0.0.0 12.0.0.2

Static Routes for Router2 are given below:

Router(config)#ip route 192.168.1.0 255.255.255.0 12.0.0.1

Router(config)#ip route 11.0.0.0 255.0.0.0 12.0.0.1

Router(config)#ip route 12.0.0.0 255.0.0.0 12.0.0.1

Router(config)#ip route 192.168.2.0 255.255.255.0 12.0.0.1

Step 5: Verifying the network by pinging the IP address of any PC. We will use the ping command to do so.

- First, click on PC0 then Go to the command prompt
- Example: ping 192.168.2.2
- Then type ping <IP address of targeted node>
- As we can see in the below image we are getting replies which means the connection is working very fine.

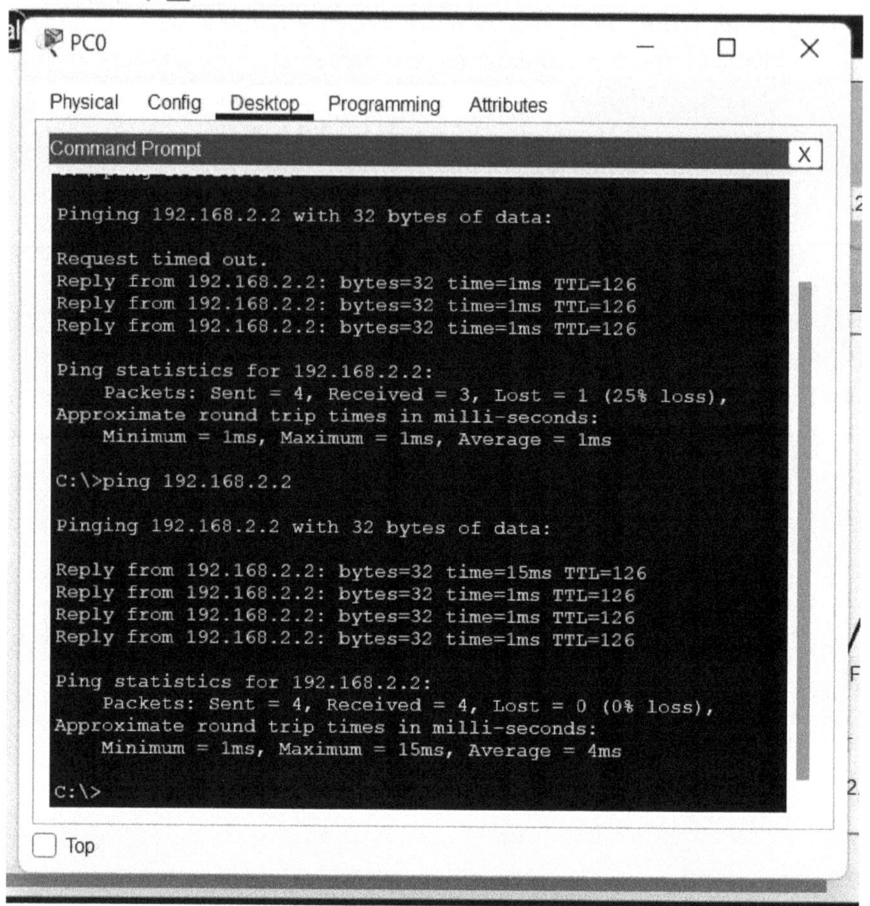

- A simulation of the experiment is given below we are sending PDU from PC0 to PC3 and PC2 to PC4:

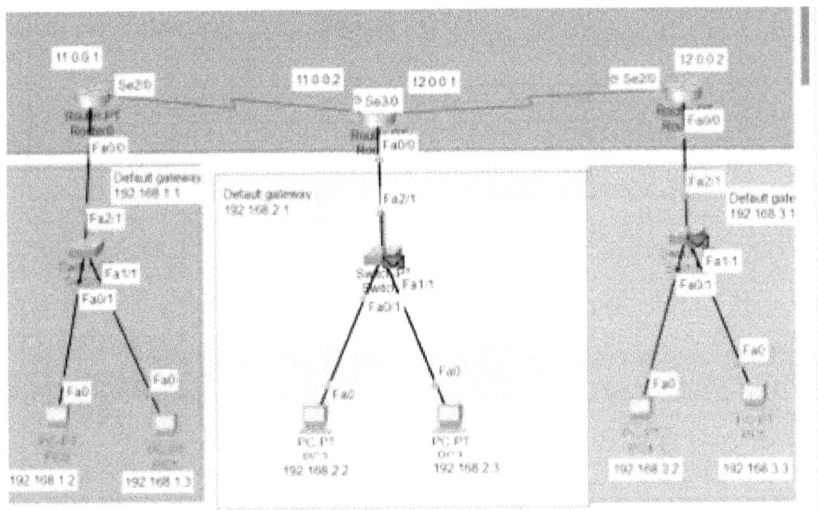

Bus, Star, mesh, ring and Hybrid topology using cisco packet tracer.

BUS : A bus topology is a network in which nodes are directly linked with a common half-duplex link. A host on a bus topology is called a station. In a bus network, every station will accept all network packets, and these packets generated by each station have equal information priority. A bus network includes a single network segment and collision domain.

Steps to Configure and Setup Bus Topology in Cisco Packet Tracer :

Step 1: First, open the cisco packet tracer desktop and select the devices given below:

- **Device - Model-Name**
  PC - PC
  Switch - PT-Switch

S.NO	Device	IPv4 Address	Subnet Mask
	pc0	192.168.0.1	255.255.255.0
	pc1	192.168.0.2	255.255.255.0
	pc2	192.168.0.3	255.255.255.0
	pc3	192.168.0.4	255.255.255.0

IP Addressing Table

- Then, create a network topology as shown below image:
- Use an Automatic connecting cable to connect the devices with others.

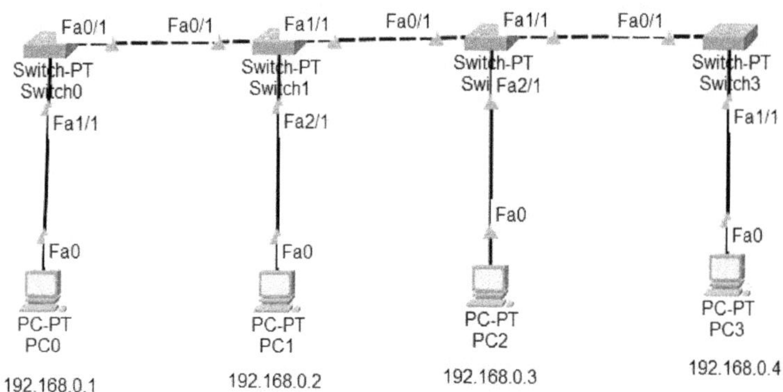

Step 2: Configure the PCs (hosts) with IPv4 address and Subnet Mask according to the IP addressing table given above.

- To assign an IP address in PC0, click on PC0.
- Then, go to desktop and then IP configuration and there you will IPv4 configuration.
- Fill IPv4 address and subnet mask.

- Assigning an IP address using the ipconfig command, or we can also assign an IP address with the help of a command.
- Go to the command terminal of the PC.
- Then, type ipconfig <IPv4 address><subnet mask><default gateway>(if needed)

Example: ipconfig 192.168.0.1 255.255.255.0

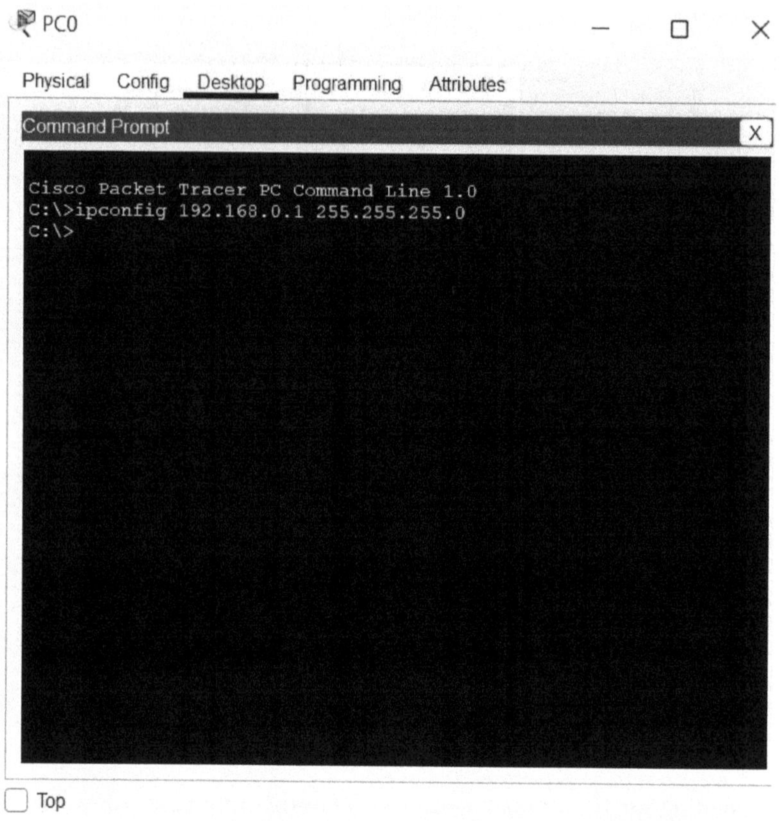

- Repeat the same procedure with other PCs to configure them thoroughly.

Step 3: Verify the connection by pinging the IP address of any host in PC0.

- Use the ping command to verify the connection.
- As we can see we are getting replies from a targeted node on both PCs.

Hence the connection is verified.

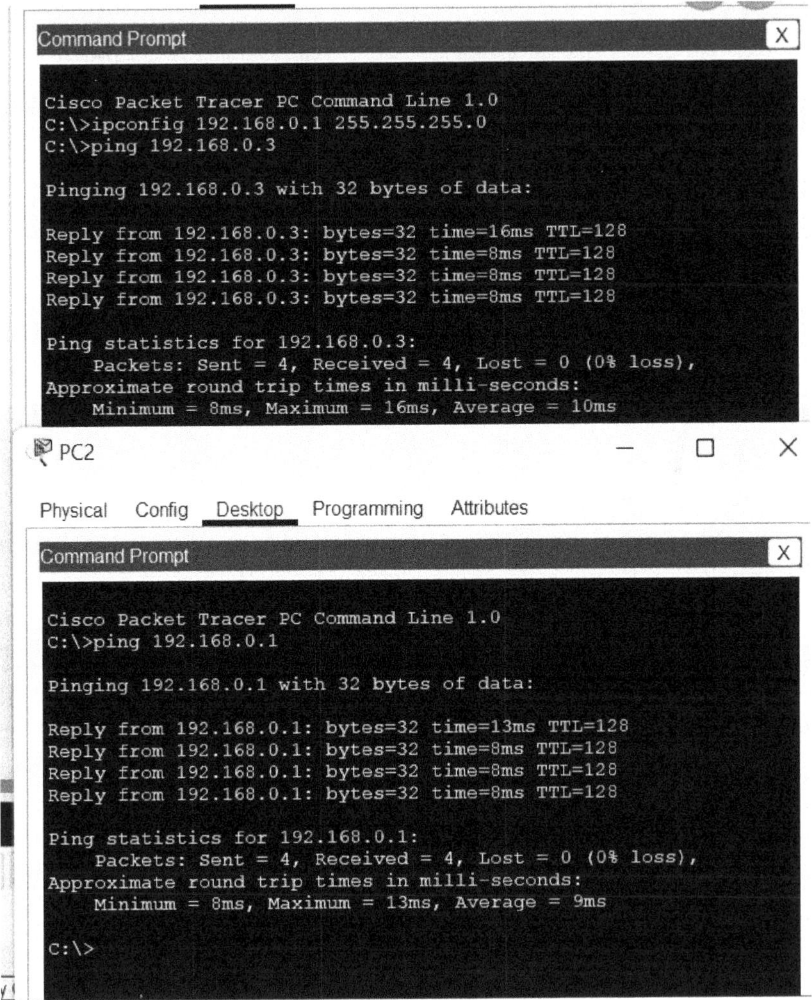

Simulation Result: A simulation of the experiment is given below we have sent two PDU packets one targeted from PC0 to PC2 and another targeted from PC3 to PC1.

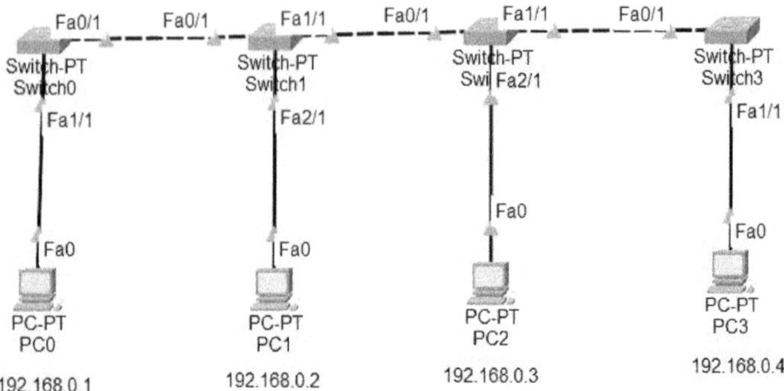

STAR:A star topology for a Local Area Network (LAN) is one in which each node is connected to a central connection point, such as a hub or switch. Whenever a node tries to connect with another node then the transmission of the message must be happening with the help of the central node. The best part of star topology is the addition and removal of the node in the network but too many nodes can cause suffering to the network.

In this article, we will discuss How to Implement Star Topology using Cisco Packet Tracer.

A Cisco packet tracer is a simulation tool that is used for understanding the networks. The best part of the Cisco packet tracer is its visualization you can see the actual flow of the message and understand the workflow of the network devices. Implementation of Star Topology using Cisco Packet Tracer is done using Switch.

Steps Implementing Star Topology using Cisco Packet Tracer:

Step 1: We have taken a switch and linked it to six end devices.

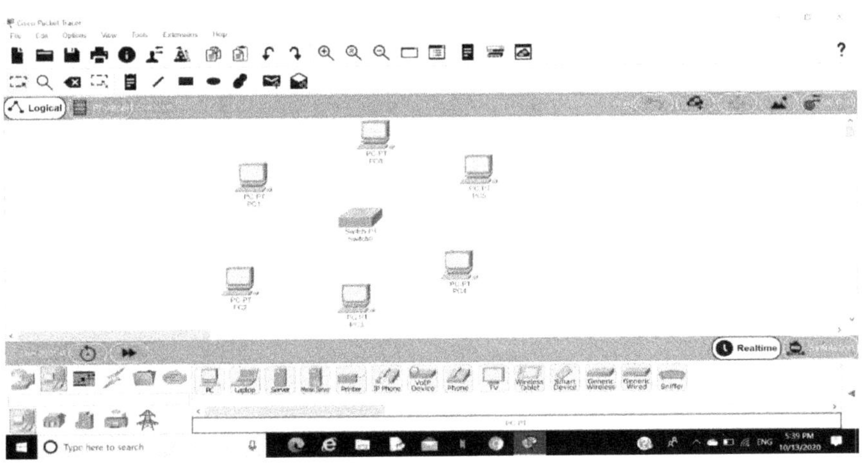

Step 2: Link every device with the switch.

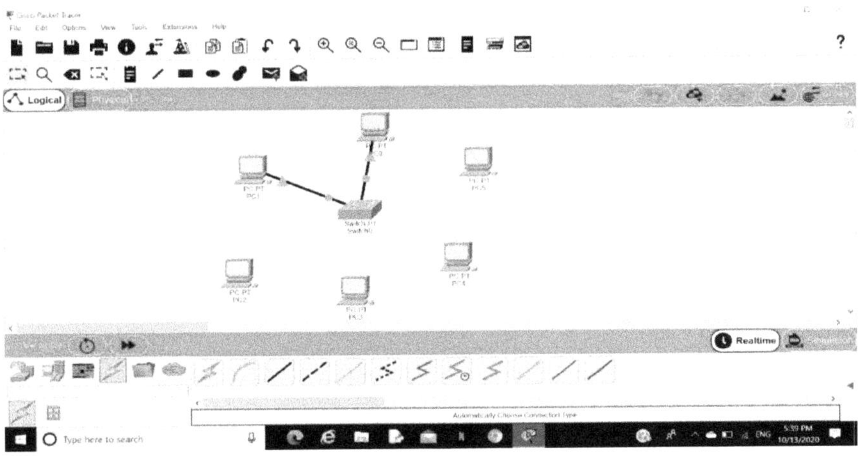

Step 3: Provide the IP address to each device.

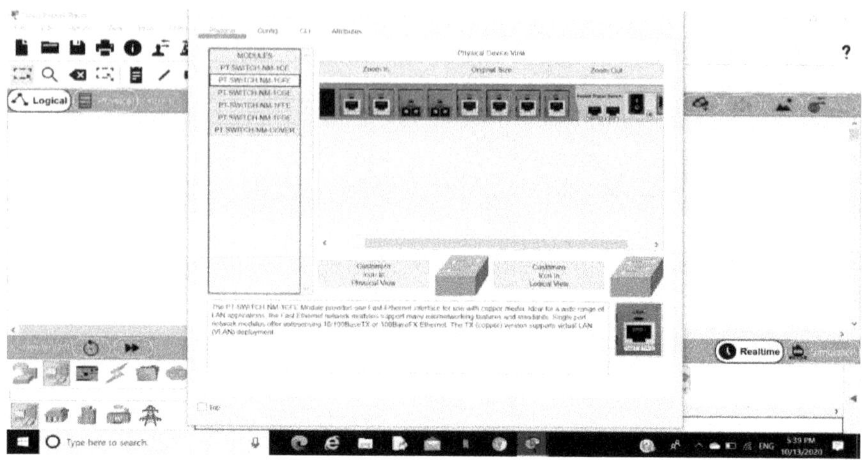

Step 4: Transfer message from one device to another and check the Table for Validation.

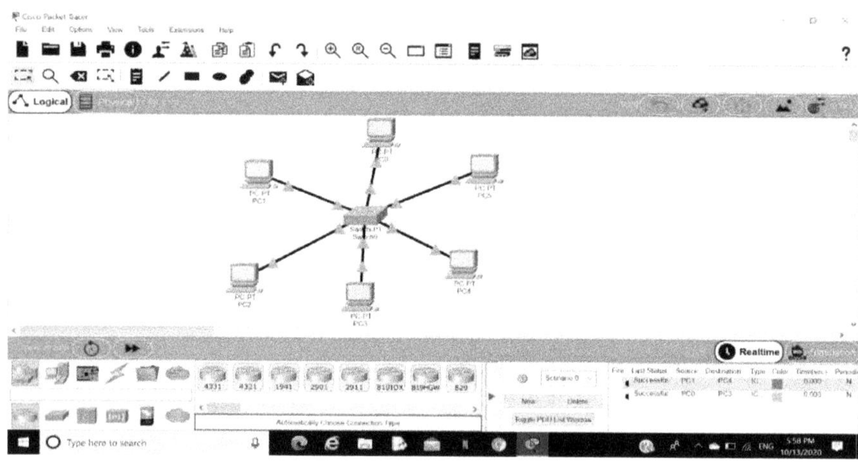

Now to check whether the connections are correct or not try to ping any device and the image below is doing the same.

To do ping one terminal of one device and run the following command:

Command:

"ping ip_address_of _any_device"

Example:

ping 192.168.1.4

Note:If the connections are correct, then you will receive the response.

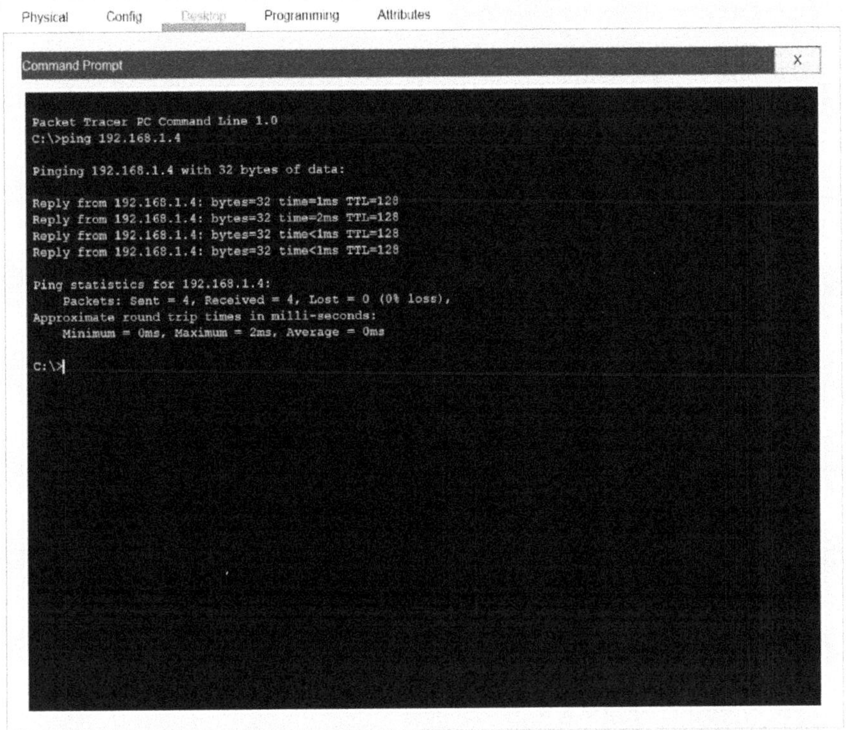

Analyze working of WI-FI and WI-MAX.

WiFi:

WiFi stands for Wireless Fidelity. WiFi uses Radio waves to provide wireless high-speed internet and network connections. A WiFi connection is established using a wireless adapter to create hotspots. WiFi antennas size is small enough to be placed on a very small router. WiFi can be used to connect with a printer, computers, gaming consoles, and many more.

WiMAX:

WiMAX stands for Wireless Inter-operability for Microwave Access.

WiMAX uses licensed or unlicensed spectrum to deliver the connection to the network. WiMAX handles a larger inter-operable network. WiMAX can be used to provide internet services such as mobile data and WiFi spots.

Difference between WiFi and WiMax:

Sr. No.	Parameters	WiFi	WiMax
1.	Defined	WiFi is defined under IEEE 802.11x standards where x stands for various WiFi versions.	WiMAX is defined under IEEE 802.16y standards where y stands for various WiMAX versions.
2.	Type of Network	WiFi is for LAN (Local Area Network) applications.	WiMAX is for MAN (Metropolitan Area Network) applications.
3.	Guarantee	WiFi does not guarantee any Quality of Service (QoS).	WiMAX guarantees Quality of Service (QoS).
4.	Distance	The WiFi network range is around 100 meters.	WiMAX network can reach about 50-90 km.
5.	Connection oriented	WiFi uses the conflict-based CSMA/CA protocol which is not connection-oriented.	WiMAX networks operate on a connection-oriented MAC.
6.	Range	WiFi is short-range technology.	WiMAX is long-range technology.
7.	Transmit	WiFi connection can transmit up to 54 Mbps.	WiMAX connection can transmit up to 70 Mbps.
8.	Signal	WiFi access points transmit signals to the receiving device.	A signal will be sent from the WiMAX base station or tower station to the WiMAX receiver.
9.	Cost	It is inexpensive compared to WiMAX technology.	It is expensive because of high installation cost.
10.	Usage	WiFi is utilized for domestic use and short-distance connections.	WiMAX supports a broader interoperable network

Describe working of Wireshark.

What is Wireshark?

- Wireshark is an open-source packet analyzer, which is used for **education, analysis, software development, communication protocol development, and network troubleshooting.**
- It is used to track the packets so that each one is filtered to meet our specific needs. It is commonly called as a **sniffer, network protocol analyzer, and network analyzer**. It is also used by network security engineers to examine security problems.
- Wireshark is a free to use application which is used to apprehend the data back and forth. It is often called as a free packet sniffer computer application. It puts the network card into an unselective mode, i.e., to accept all the packets which it receives.

Uses of Wireshark: Wireshark can be used in the following ways:

- It is used by network security engineers to examine security problems.
- It allows the users to watch all the traffic being passed over the network.
- It is used by network engineers to troubleshoot network issues.
- It also helps to troubleshoot latency issues and malicious activities on your network.
- It can also analyze dropped packets.
- It helps us to know how all the devices like laptop, mobile phones, desktop, switch, routers, etc., communicate in a local network or the rest of the world.

What is a packet?

- A packet is a unit of data which is transmitted over a network between the origin and the destination. Network packets are small, i.e., maximum **1.5 Kilobytes for Ethernet packets and 64 Kilobytes for IP packets**. The data packets in the Wireshark can be viewed online and can be analyzed offline.
- **History of Wireshark:** In the late 1990's **Gerald Combs**, a computer

science graduate of the University of Missouri-Kansas City was working for the small ISP (Internet Service Provider). The protocol at that time did not complete the primary requirements. So, he started writing **ethereal** and released the first version around 1998. The Network integration services owned the Ethernet trademark.

- Combos still held the copyright on most of the ethereal source code, and the rest of the source code was re-distributed under the GNU GPL. He did not own the Ethereal trademark, so he changed the name to Wireshark. He used the contents of the ethereal as the basis.
- Wireshark has won several industry rewards over the years including eWeek, InfoWorld, PC Magazine and also as a top-rated packet sniffer. Combos continued the work and released the new version of the software. There are around 600 contributed authors for the Wireshark product website.

Functionality of Wireshark:

- Wireshark is similar to tcpdump in networking. **Tcpdump** is a common packet analyzer which allows the user to display other packets and TCP/IP packets, being transmitted and received over a network attached to the computer. It has a graphic end and some sorting and filtering functions. Wireshark users can see all the traffic passing through the network.
- Wireshark can also monitor the unicast traffic which is not sent to the network's MAC address interface. But, the switch does not pass all the traffic to the port. Hence, the promiscuous mode is not sufficient to see all the traffic. The various network taps or **port mirroring** is used to extend capture at any point.
- Port mirroring is a method to monitor network traffic. When it is enabled, the switch sends the copies of all the network packets present at one port to another port.

What is color coding in Wireshark?

- The packets in the Wireshark are highlighted with **blue**, **black**, and **green color**. These colors help users to identify the types of traffic. It is also called as **packet colorization**. The kinds of coloring rules in the Wireshark are **temporary rules** and **permanent rules**.

- The temporary rules are there until the program is in active mode or until we quit the program.
- The permanent color rules are available until the Wireshark is in use or the next time you run the Wireshark. The steps to apply color filters will be discussed later in this topic.

Features of Wireshark

- It is multi-platform software, i.e., it can run on Linux, Windows, OS X, FreeBSD, NetBSD, etc.
- It is a standard three-pane packet browser.
- It performs deep inspection of the hundreds of protocols.
- It often involves live analysis, i.e., from the different types of the network like the Ethernet, loopback, etc., we can read live data.
- It has sort and filter options which makes ease to the user to view the data.
- It is also useful in VoIP analysis.
- It can also capture raw USB traffic.
- Various settings, like timers and filters, can be used to filter the output.
- It can only capture packet on the PCAP (an application programming interface used to capture the network) supported networks.
- Wireshark supports a variety of well-documented capture file formats such as the PcapNg and Libpcap. These formats are used for storing the captured data.
- It is the no.1 piece of software for its purpose. It has countless applications ranging from the **tracing down, unauthorized traffic, firewall settings, etc.**

Installation of Wireshark Software

Below are the steps to install the Wireshark software on the computer:

- Open the web browser.
- Search for '**Download Wireshark.**'
- Select the Windows installer according to your system configuration, either 32-bt or 64-bit. Save the program and close the browser.
- Now, open the software, and follow the install instruction by accepting the license.
- The Wireshark is ready for use.

- On the network and Internet settings option, we can check the interface connected to our computer.
- If you are Linux users, then you will find Wireshark in its package repositories.
- By selecting the current interface, we can get the traffic traversing through that interface. The version used here is **3.0.3**. This version will open as:

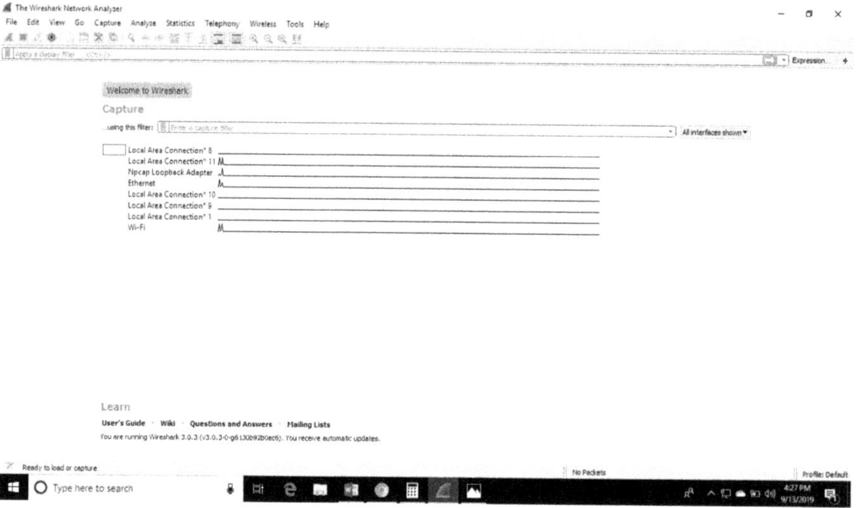

The Wireshark software window is shown above, and all the processes on the network are carried within this screen only.

The options given on the list are the Interface list options. The number of interface options will be present. Selection of any option will determine all the traffic. **For example,** from the above fig. select the Wi-Fi option. After this, a new window opens up, which will show all the current traffic on the network. Below is the image which tells us about the live capture of packets and our Wireshark will look like:

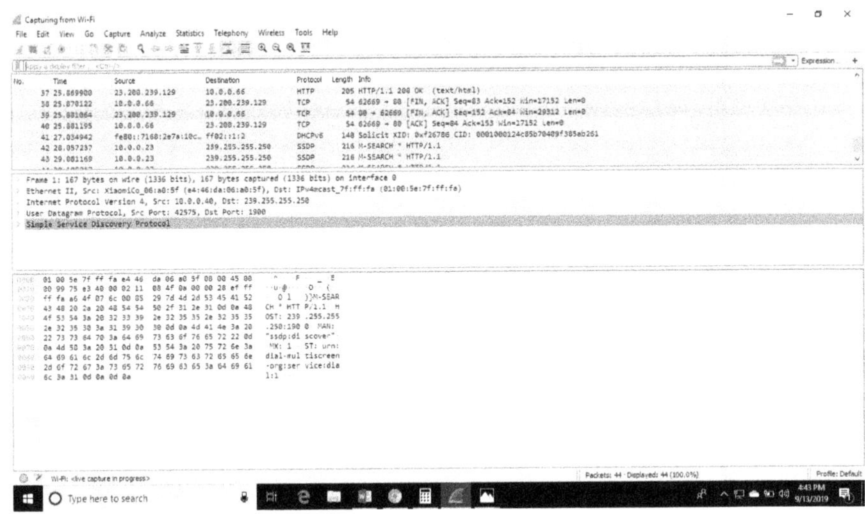

The above arrow shows the packet content written in hexadecimal or the ASCII format. And the information above the packet content, are the details of the packet header.

It will continue listening to all the data packets, and you will get much data. If you want to see a particular data, then you can click on the red button. The traffic will be stationary, and you can note the parameters like time, source, destination, the protocol being used, length, and the Info. To view in-depth detail, you can click on that particular address; a lot of the information will be displayed below that.

There will be detailed information on HTTP packets, TCP packets, etc. The red button is shown below:

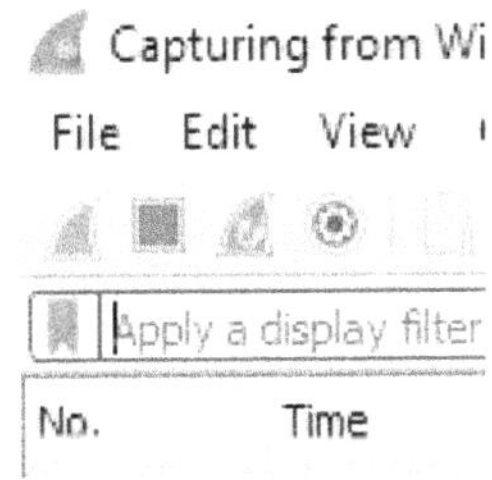

The screen/interface of the Wireshark is divided into five parts:

- First part contains a menu bar and the options displayed below it. This part is at the top of the window. File and the capture menus options are commonly used in Wireshark. The capture menu allows to start the capturing process. And the File menu is used to open and save a capture file.
- The second part is the packet listing window. It determines the packet flow or the captured packets in the traffic. It includes the packet number, time, source, destination, protocol, length, and info. We can sort the packet list by clicking on the column name.
- Next comes the packet header- detailed window. It contains detailed information about the components of the packets. The protocol info can also be expanded or minimized according to the information required.
- The bottom window called the packet contents window, which displays the content in ASCII and hexadecimal format.
- At last, is the filter field which is at the top of the display. The captured packets on the screen can be filtered based on any component according to your requirements. For example, if we want to see only the packets with the HTTP protocol, we can apply filters to that option. All the packets with HTTP as the protocol will only be displayed on the screen, shown below:

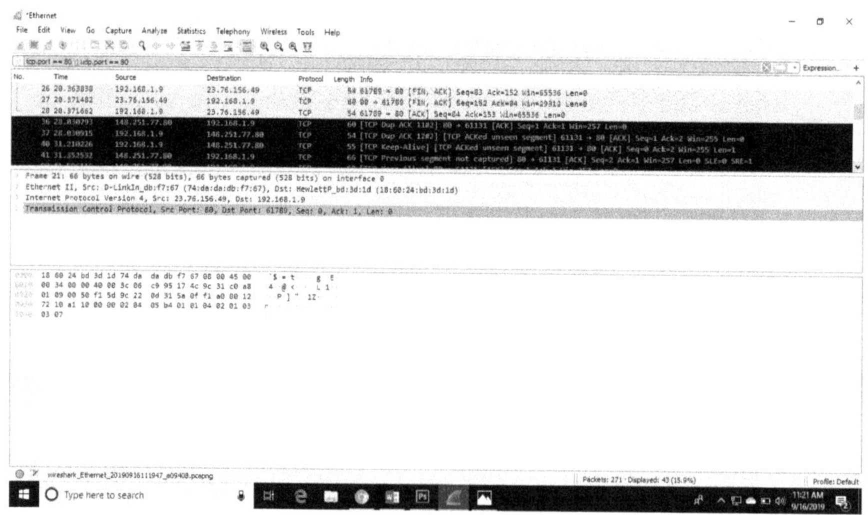

You can also select the connection to which your computer is connected. For example, in this PC, we have chosen the current network, i.e., the ETHERNET.

After connecting, you can watch the traffic below:

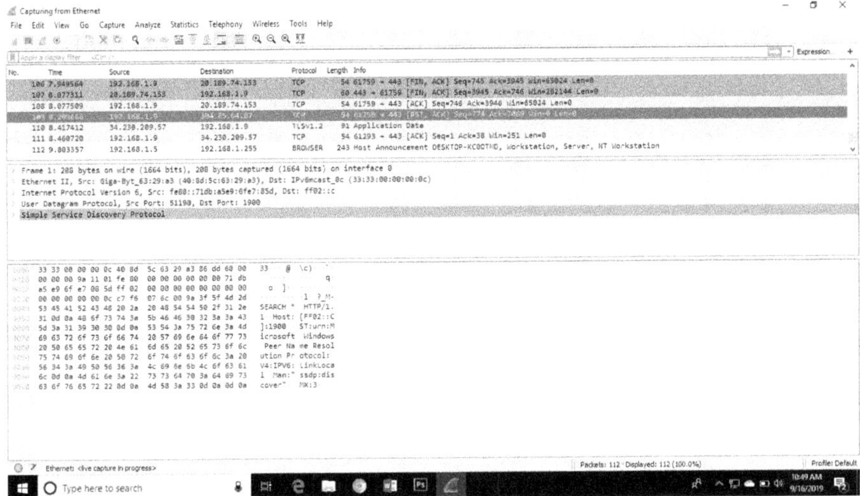

In view option on the menu bar, we can also change the view of the interface. You can change the number of things in the view menu. You can also enable or disable any option according to the requirements.

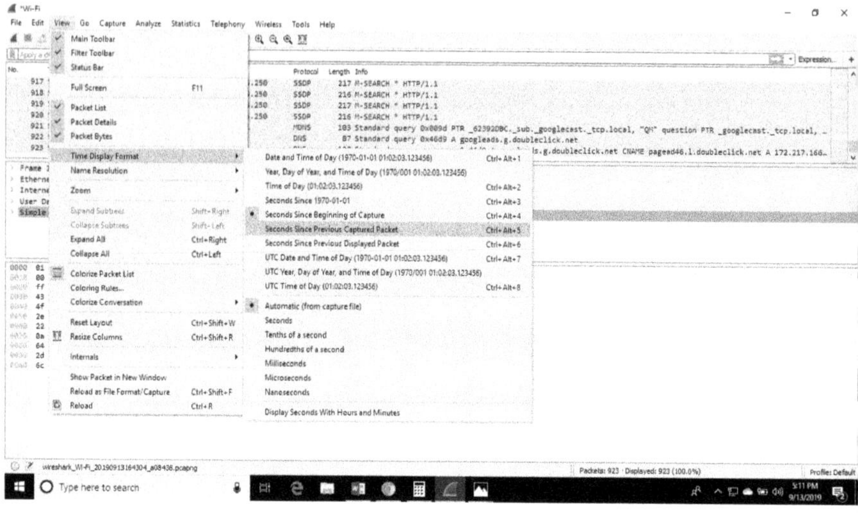

There is a filter block below the menu bar, from where a large amount of data can be filtered. For example, if we apply a filter for HTTP, only the interfaces with the HTTP will be listed.

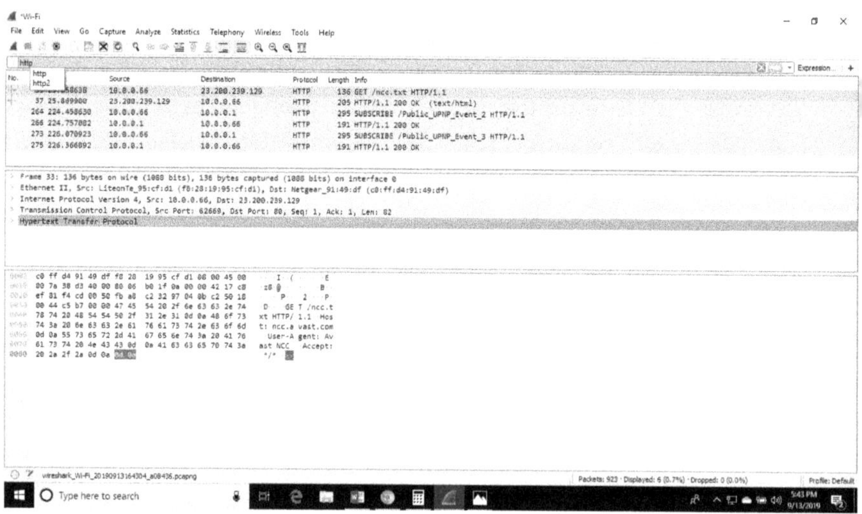

If you want to filter according to the source, right-click on the source you want to filter and select 'Apply as Filter' and choose '...and filter.'

Steps for the permanent colorization are: click on the 'View' option on the menu bar and select 'Coloring Rules.' The table will appear like the image shown below:

For the network administrator job, advanced knowledge of Wireshark is considered as the requirements. So, it is essential to understand the concepts of the software. It contains these 20 default coloring rules which can be added or removed according to the requirements.

Select the option '**View**' and then choose '**Colorize Packet List**,' which is used to **toggle the color on and off.**

Packet capture and Protocol Analyzer using Wireshark.

Wireshark for Linux

Installing Wireshark on Linux can be a little different depending on the Linux distribution. If you aren't running one of the following distros, please double-check the commands.

Ubuntu

From a Terminal prompt, run these commands:

- **sudo apt-get install wireshark**
- **sudo dpkg-reconfigure wireshark-common**
- **sudo adduser $USER wireshark**

Those commands download and update the package, and add user privileges to run Wireshark.

Red Hat Fedora

From a Terminal prompt, run these commands:

- **sudo dnf install wireshark-qt**
- **sudo usermod -a -G wireshark username**

The first command installs the GUI and CLI version of Wireshark, and the second adds permissions to use Wireshark.

Kali Linux

Wireshark is probably already installed because it's part of the basic package. Check your menu under the option "Sniffing & Spoofing" to verify.

Data packets on Wireshark: Now that we hNormalave Wireshark installed, let's go over how to enable the Wireshark packet sniffer and then analyze the network traffic.

Go beyond the wire with your security.

Wireshark will tell you what is happening in your network traffic, but it won't tell you why.

Capturing data packets on Wireshark

When you open Wireshark, you see a screen showing you a list of all the network connections you can monitor. You also have a capture filter field to only capture the network traffic you want to see.

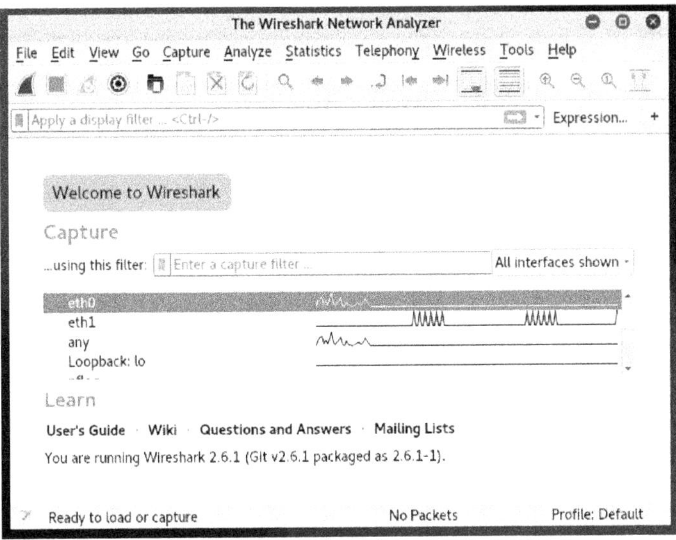

You can select one or more of the network interfaces using shift+left-click. Once select the network interface, you can start the capture, and there are several ways to do that.

Click the first button on the toolbar, titled "Start capturing packets."

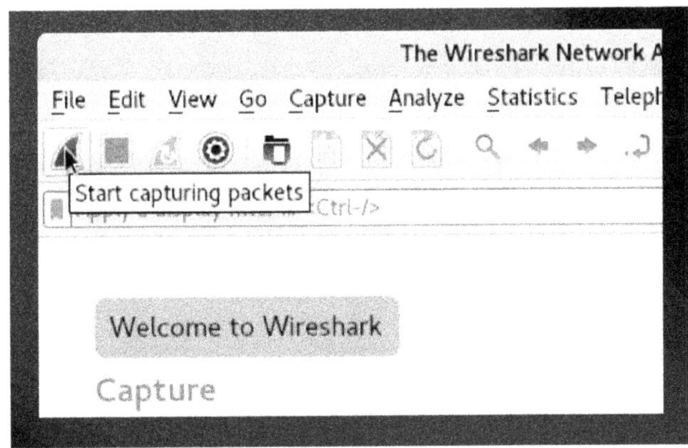

You can select the menu item Capture -> Start.

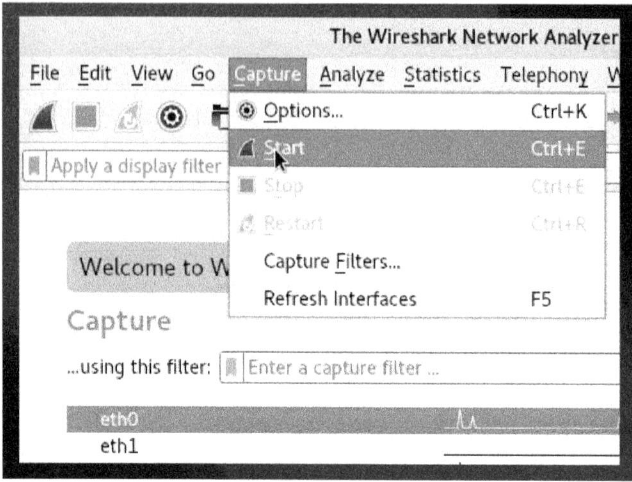

Or you could use the keystroke Control+E.

During the capture, Wireshark will show you the packets captured in real-time.

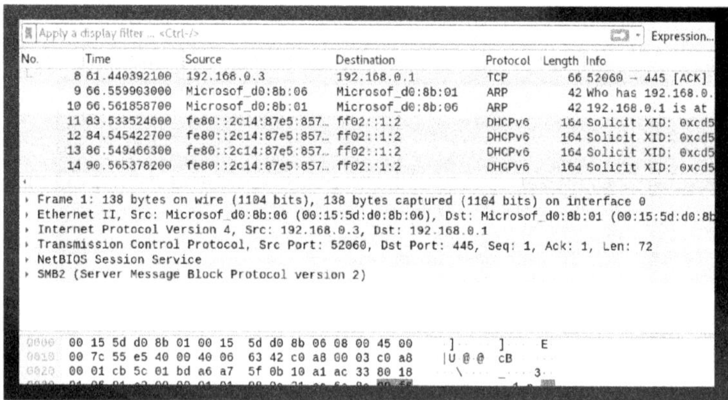

the capture as you did to begin.

Best practice dictates stopping Wireshark's packet capture before analysis.

Analyzing data packets on Wireshark: Wireshark shows you three different panes for inspecting packet data. The Packet List, the top pane, lists all the packets in the capture. When you click on a packet, the other two panes change to show you the details about the selected packet. You can also tell if the packet is part of a conversation. Here are details about each column in the top pane:

- **No.**: This is the number order of the packet captured. The bracket indicates that this packet is part of a conversation.
- **Time**: This column shows how long after you started the capture this particular packet was captured. You can change this value in the Settings menu to display a different option.
- **Source**: This is the address of the system that sent the packet.
- **Destination**: This is the address of the packet destination.
- **Protocol**: This is the type of packet. For example: TCP, DNS, DHCPv6, or ARP.
- **Length**: This column shows you the packet's length, measured in bytes.
- **Info**: This column shows you more information about the packet contents, which will vary depending on the type of packet.

Packet Details, the middle pane, shows you as much readable information about the packet as possible, depending on the packet type. You can right-click and create filters based on the highlighted text in this field.

The bottom pane, Packet Bytes, displays the packet exactly as it was captured in hexadecimal.

When looking at a packet that is part of a conversation, you can right-click the packet and select Follow to see only the packets that are part of that conversation.

Wireshark filters: Some of the best features of Wireshark are the capture filters and display filters. Filters allow you to view the capture the way you need to see it to troubleshoot the issues at hand. Below are several filters to get you started.

Wireshark capture filters

Capture filters limit the captured packets by the chosen filter. If the packets don't match the filter, Wireshark won't save them. Examples of capture filters include:

host IP-*address*: This filter limits the captured traffic to and from the IP address

net 192.168.0.0/24: This filter captures all traffic on the subnet

dst host IP-*address*: Capture packets sent to the specified host

port 53: Capture traffic on port 53 only

port not 53 and not arp: Capture all traffic except DNS and ARP traffic

Wireshark display filters: Wireshark display filters change the view of the capture during analysis. After you've stopped the packet capture, use display filters to narrow down the packets in the Packet List to troubleshoot your issue.

One of the most useful display filters is:

ip.src==*IP-address* and ip.dst==*IP-address*

This filter shows packets sent from one computer (ip.src) to another (ip.dst). You can also use ip.addr to show packets to and from that IP. Other filters include:

tcp.port eq 25: This filter will show you all traffic on port 25, which is usually SMTP traffic

icmp: This filter will show you only ICMP traffic in the capture, most likely they are pings

ip.addr != *IP_address*: This filter shows you all traffic except the traffic to or from the specified computer

Analysts even build filters to detect specific attacks, like this filter used to detect the Sasser worm:

ls_ads.opnum==0x09

Additional Wireshark features: Beyond the capture and filtering, several other features in Wireshark can make your job easier.

Capturing Password using Wireshark.

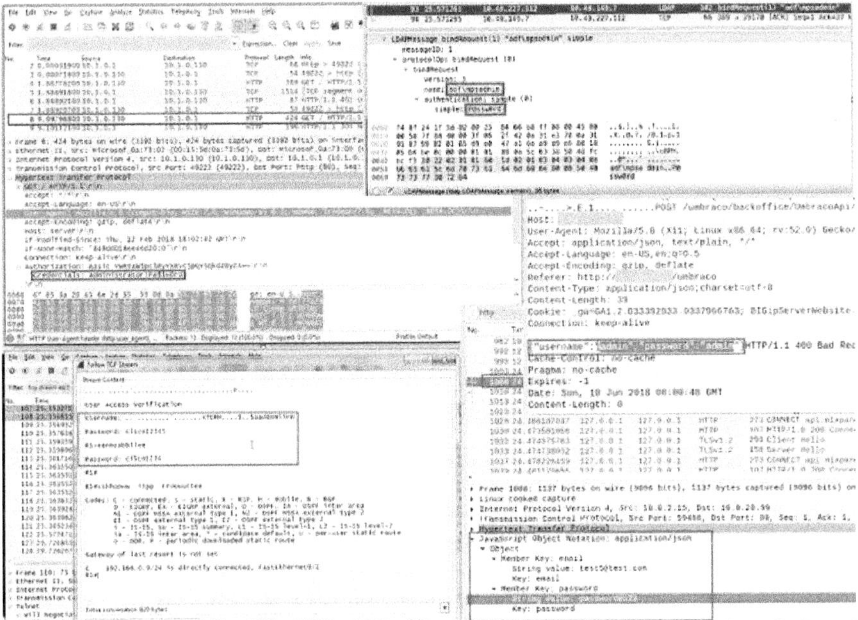

Many people ask this question: Can Wireshark capture passwords? Well, the answer is definitely yes! Wireshark can capture not only passwords, but any kind of information passing through the network – usernames, email addresses, personal information, pictures, videos, anything. As long as we are in position to capture network traffic, Wireshark can sniff the passwords going through.

Plain text network protocols: So how is it actually possible that Wireshark can capture passwords? That's because some network protocols do not use encryption. Such protocols are called clear text (or plain text) protocols. And since clear text protocols do not encrypt the communication, all data are visible to the naked eye, including passwords. Anybody who is in position to see the communication (e.g. man in the middle) can ultimately see everything.

Following table lists some of the most popular clear text protocols still being used today and also some other protocols which allow clear text authentication:

Port	Service	Name
tcp/20, tcp/21	FTP	File Transfer Protocol
tcp/23	Telnet	Teletype Network Protocol
tcp/25	SMTP	Simple Mail Transfer Protocol
tcp/80	HTTP	Hyper Text Transfer Protocol
tcp/110	POP3	Post Office Protocol
tcp/143	IMAP4	Internet Message Access Protocol
udp/161, udp/162	SNMP	Simple Network Management Protocol
tcp/389	LDAP	Lightweight Directory Access Protocol
tcp/1080	SOCKS	SOCKetS Proxy Protocol
tcp/1433	MSSQL	Microsoft SQL Database
tcp/5222	XMPP	Extensible Messaging and Presence Protocol (Jabber)
tcp/5432	PostgreSQL	PostgreSQL Database
tcp/6667	IRC	Internet Relay Chat

In the following sections we will look closer on these protocols and see examples of captured passwords using Wireshark.

Disclaimer: All screenshots has been redacted and/or modified to protect client data.

Capture FTP password: File Transfer Protocol (FTP) was born in 1971 and it typically uses ports tcp/20, tcp/21. Although it is very old protocol, some organizations still use it today in their networks. FTP is a plain text protocol and therefore a well positioned attacker can capture FTP login credentials very easily using Wireshark. The following screenshot shows example of a captured FTP password using Wireshark:

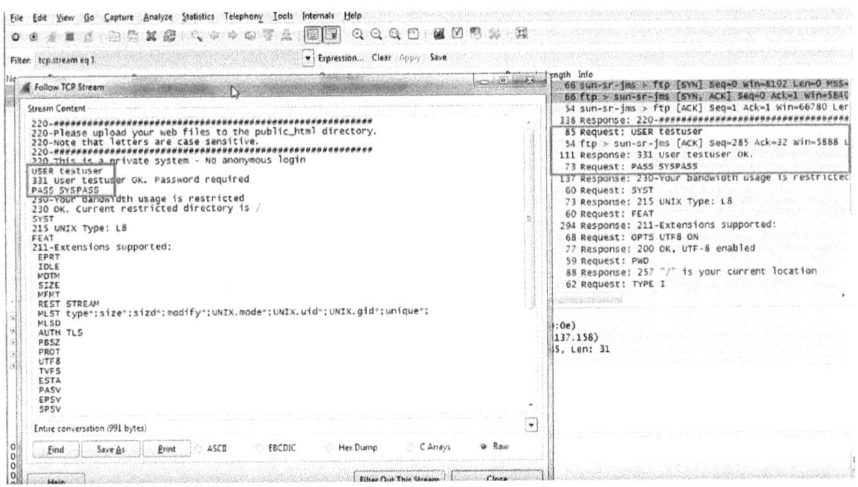

Extract files from FTP using Wireshark: Since FTP is a plain text protocol, we can also capture the actual data being transferred over this protocol. We can extract all the files (e.g. images, documents, audio files etc.) from the network with Wireshark. Brad Duncan from PaloAlto Networks wrote an excellent article describing how to do that.

We could also use Chaosreader to extract the data out from a PCAP file.

Capture Telnet password: Telnet protocol using port tcp/23 certainly needs no introduction. It is used mainly for administration purposes and it is notoriously known for its insecurity. Because there is no encryption, there is no privacy nor protection against eavesdropping. Nevertheless, Telnet is still being used today.

There are many different devices that use telnet as a protocol for administration. For some devices, telnet is the only option without having any alternative (e.g. there is no SSH nor HTTPS web interface available). This makes it very hard for the organizations to get rid of it completely. Telnet can be usually seen on:

- Network equipment (routers, switches..)
- Video conferencing systems (e.g. Cisco TelePresence)
- Access control systems (e.g. access card readers)
- Storage and tape systems
- Printers and imaging devices

- Legacy IP phones
- Mainframes

Since telnet is a plain text protocol, a well positioned adversary can eavesdrop on the communication and capture everything, including passwords. Example of a telnet communication with captured password can be seen in the following screenshot:

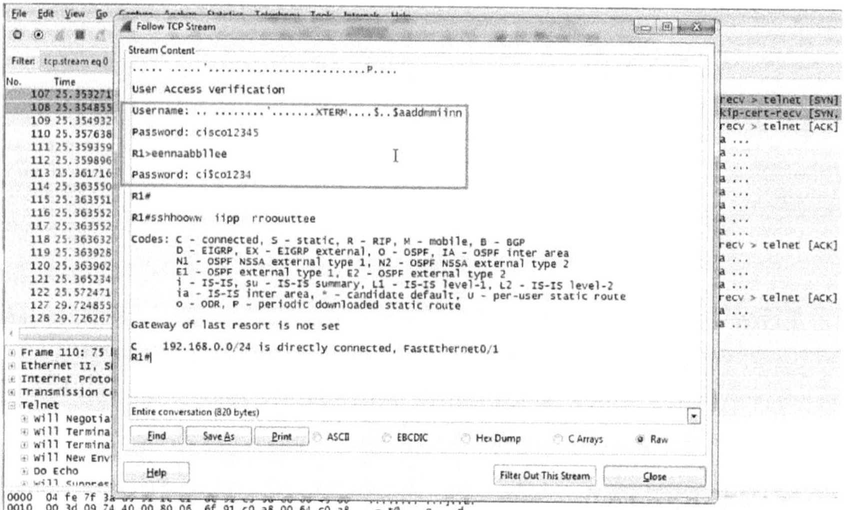

An attacker could now completely overtake the Cisco router.

Capture SMTP password: Simple Mail Transfer Protocol (SMTP) has also been with us for many decades. It uses port tcp/25 and although there is a secure alternative on port tcp/464, the port tcp/25 is open practically on every mail server today due to the backward compatibility.

Most of the servers on port tcp/25 require 'STARTTLS' command to initiate the SSL/TLS encryption before any authentication attempts. However, mail servers within some organizations still support plain text authentication over the unencrypted channel. This is mostly due to legacy systems within their internal networks.

If somebody uses a plain text authentication during SMTP transaction, a well positioned attacker can sniff the credentials. All that the attacker has to do is to base64 decode the username and password. That is because SMTP uses base64 encoding to encode the username and password during the transaction.

In the following screenshot we can see a captured SMTP credentials using Wireshark and consequent base64 decoding using the base64 utility on Linux:

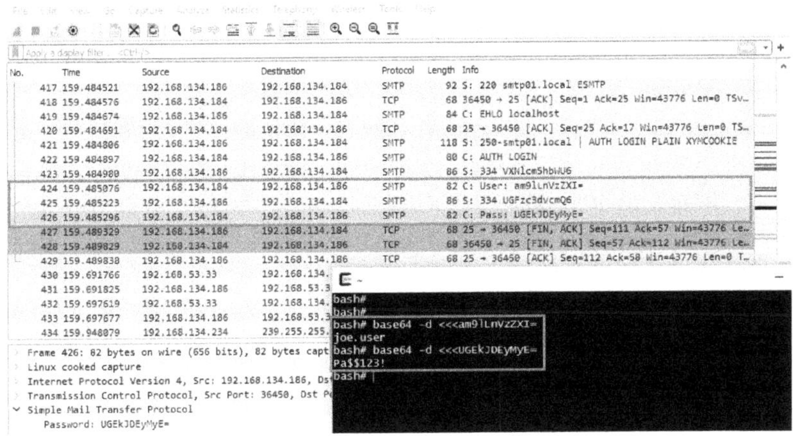

On Windows we could use the certutil.exe command to decode the captured credentials like this:

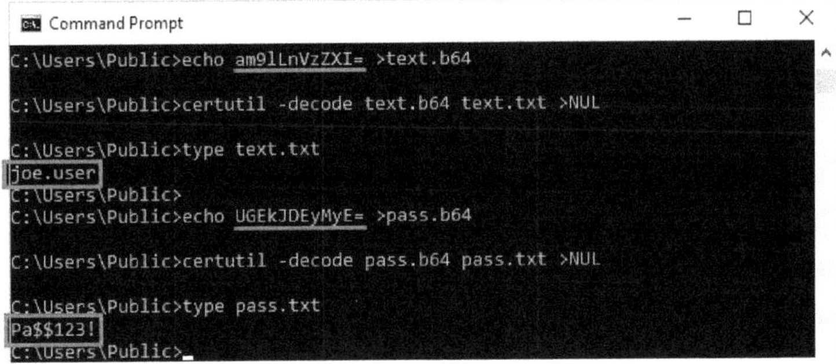

Note that we could also use online tools such as base64decode.org or base64decode.net to do the base64 decoding. But we should be careful with this – perhaps we don't want to be disclosing private credentials to other parties on the Internet. This is especially important during penetration tests and other offensive exercises, where sensitivity and privacy is crucial.

Configure SNMP using relevant software.

Introduction: This document describes how to configure Simple Network Management Protocol strings on Cisco routers, Route Switch Modules, and Catalyst switches.

Background: This document describes how to configure Simple Network Management Protocol (SNMP) community strings on Cisco routers, Route Switch Modules (RSMs), and Catalyst switches. In the context of this document, configure is defined as verify, enable, modify, and disable SNMP community strings.

Prerequisites

Requirements

There are no specific requirements for this document.

Components Used

The information in this document was created from the devices in a specific lab environment. All of the devices used in this document started with a cleared (default) configuration. If your network is live, ensure that you understand the potential impact of any command.

This document is not restricted to specific software and hardware versions.

Conventions

Refer to the Cisco Technical Tips Conventions for more information on document conventions.

Configurate SNMP on Router and Catalyst Switch

Enable SNMP Community Strings

This procedure is the same for both routers and Cisco IOS® software-based XL Catalyst Switches.

1. Telnet to the router:

prompt# **telnet 172.16.99.20**

2. Enter the enable password at the prompt in order to enter the enable mode:

Router>**enable**

Password:

Router#

3. Display the running configuration and look for the SNMP information:

Router#**show running-config**

Building configuration...

Note: If no SNMP information is present, continue with these steps. If any SNMP commands are listed, you can modify or disable them.

4. Go into the configuration mode:

Router#**configure terminal**

Enter configuration commands, one per line. End with CNTL/Z.

Router(config)#

5. Use this command in order to enable the read-only (RO) community string:

Router(config)#**snmp-server community public RO**

where "public" is the read-only community string.

6. Use this command in order to enable the read-write (RW) community string:

Router(config)#**snmp-server community private RW**

where "private" is the read-write community string.

7. Exit out of the configuration mode and return to the main prompt:

Router(config)#**exit**

Router#

8. Write the modified configuration to nonvolatile RAM (NVRAM) to save the settings:

Router#**write memory**

Building configuration...

[OK]

Router#

Verify SNMP Community Strings

Follow these steps to verify SNMP community strings.

1. Verify that there is TCP/IP connectivity between the Network Management Server (NMS) server and the router

C:\>**ping 172.16.99.20**

Pinging 172.16.99.20 with 32 bytes of data:

Reply from 172.16.99.20: bytes=32 time<10ms TTL=247

Reply from 172.16.99.20: bytes=32 time=10ms TTL=247

Reply from 172.16.99.20: bytes=32 time<10ms TTL=247

Reply from 172.16.99.20: bytes=32 time<10ms TTL=247

Ping statistics for 172.16.99.20:

Packets: Sent = 4, Received = 4, Lost = 0 (0% loss),

Approximate round trip times in milli-seconds:

Minimum = 0ms, Maximum = 10ms, Average = 2ms

2. Telnet to the router:

prompt# **telnet 172.16.99.20**

3. Enter the enable password at the prompt in order to enter the enable mode:

Router>**enable**

Password:

Router#

4. Display the running configuration and look for the SNMP information:

Router#**show running-config**

....

snmp-server community public RO

snmp-server community private RW

....

In this sample output, "public" is the read-only community string and "private" is the read-write community string.

If no SNMP information is present, continue with these steps. If any SNMP commands are listed, you can modify or disable them.

Note: If you do not see any "snmp-server" statements, SNMP is not enabled on the router. Alternatively, execute the **show snmp** command in the enable mode. If you see this message, it also indicates that SNMP is not enabled on the router. For example:

Router#**show snmp**

%SNMP agent not enabled

Router#

5. Exit the enable mode and return to the main prompt:

Router#**disable**

Router>

Modify SNMP Community Strings

Complete these steps in order to modify SNMP community strings.

1. Telnet to the router:

prompt# **telnet 172.16.99.20**

2. Enter the enable password at the prompt in order to enter the enable mode:

Router>**enable**

Password:

Router#

3. Display the running configuration and look for the SNMP information:

Router#**show running-config**

Building configuration...

...

...

snmp-server community public RO

snmp-server community private RW

....

....

4. Go into the configuration mode:

Router#**configure terminal**

Enter configuration commands, one per line. End with CNTL/Z.

Router(config)#

Follow these steps to modify the current read-only (RO) community string:

a. Delete the current read-only (RO) community string with this command:

Router(config)#**no snmp-server community public RO**

where "public" is the read-only community string.

b. Enter the new read-only (RO) community string with this command:

Router(config)#**snmp-server community XXXX RO**

where "XXXX" is the read-only community string.

Follow these steps to modify the current read-write (RW) community string:

a. Delete the current read-write (RW) community string with this command:

Router(config)#**no snmp-server community private RW**

where "private" is the read-write (RW) community string.

b. Enter the new read-write (RW) community string with this command:

Router(config)#**snmp-server community YYYY RW**

where "YYYY" is the read-write community string.

5. Exit the configuration mode and return to the main prompt:

Router(config)#**exit**

Router#

6. Write the modified configuration to nonvolatile RAM (NVRAM) to save the settings:

Router#**write memory**

Building configuration...

[OK]

Router#

Disable/Remove SNMP Community Strings

Follow these steps to disable or remove SMMP community strings.

1. Telnet to the router:

prompt# **telnet 172.16.99.20**

2. Enter the enable password at the prompt in order to enter the enable mode:

Router>**enable**

Password:

Router#

3. Display the running configuration and look for the SNMP information:

Router#**show running-config**

Building configuration...

...

...

snmp-server community public RO

snmp-server community private RW

....

....

4. Go into the configuration mode:

Router#**configure terminal**

Enter configuration commands, one per line. End with CNTL/Z.

Router(config)#

5. In order to disable/remove the current read-only (RO) community string, use this command:

Router(config)#**no snmp-server community public RO**

where "public" is the read-only community string.

6. In order to disable/remove the current read-write (RW) community string, use this command:

Router(config)#**no snmp-server community private RW**

where "private" is the read-write community string.

7. Exit out of the configuration mode and return to the main prompt:

Router(config)#**exit**

Router#

8. Write the modified configuration to nonvolatile RAM (NVRAM) to save the settings:

Router#**write memory**

Building configuration...

[OK]

Router#

Explain working of PIM, DVMRP protocols.

PIM: Protocol Independent Multicast (PIM) is a collection of multicast routing protocols, each optimized for a different environment. There are two main PIM protocols, PIM Sparse Mode and PIM Dense Mode. A third PIM protocol, Bi-directional PIM, is less widely used.

Typically, either PIM Sparse Mode or PIM Dense Mode will be used throughout a multicast domain. However, they may also be used together within a single domain, using Sparse Mode for some groups and Dense Mode for others. This mixed-mode configuration is known as Sparse-Dense Mode. Similarly, Bi-directional PIM may be used on its own, or it may be used in conjunction with one or both of PIM Sparse Mode and PIM Dense Mode.

All PIM protocols share a common control message format. PIM control messages are sent as raw IP datagrams (protocol number 103), either multicast to the link-local ALL PIM ROUTERS multicast group, or unicast to a specific destination.

PIM Sparse Mode: PIM Sparse Mode (PIM-SM) is a multicast routing protocol designed on the assumption that recipients for any particular multicast group will be sparsely distributed throughout the network. In other words, it is assumed that most subnets in the network will not want any given multicast packet. In order to receive multicast data, routers must explicitly tell their upstream neighbors about their interest in particular groups and sources. Routers use PIM Join and Prune messages to join and leave multicast distribution trees. PIM-SM by default uses shared trees, which are multicast distribution trees rooted at some selected node (in PIM, this router is called the Rendezvous Point, or RP) and used by all sources sending to the multicast group. To send to the RP, sources must encapsulate data in PIM control messages and send it by unicast to the RP. This is done by the source's Designated Router (DR), which is a router on the source's local network. A single DR is elected from all PIM routers on a network, so that unnecessary control messages are not sent.

One of the important requirements of PIM Sparse Mode, and Bi-directional PIM, is the ability to discover the address of a RP for a multicast group using a shared tree. Various RP discovery mechanisms are used, including static configuration, Bootstrap Router, Auto-RP, Anycast RP, and Embedded RP.

PIM-SM also supports the use of source-based trees, in which a separate multicast distribution tree is built for each source sending data to a multicast group. Each tree is rooted at a router adjacent to the source, and sources send data directly to the root of the tree. Source-based trees enable the use of Source-Specific Multicast (SSM), which allows hosts to specify the source from which they wish to receive data, as well as the multicast group they wish to join. With SSM, a host identifies a multicast data stream with a source and group address pair (S,G), rather than by group address alone (*,G).

PIM-SM may use source-based trees in the following circumstances.

- For SSM, a last-hop router will join a source-based tree from the outset.
- To avoid data sent to an RP having to be encapsulated, the RP may join a source-based tree.
- To optimize the data path, a last-hop router may choose to switch from the shared tree to a source-based tree.

PIM-SM is a soft-state protocol. That is, all state is timed-out a while after receiving the control message that instantiated it. To keep the state alive, all PIM Join messages are periodically retransmitted.

Version 1 of PIM-SM was created in 1995, but was never standardized by the IETF. It is now considered obsolete, though it is still supported by Cisco and Juniper routers. Version 2 of PIM-SM was standardized in RFC 2117 (in 1997) and updated by RFC 2362 (in 1998). Version 2 is significantly different from and incompatible with version 1. However, there were a number of problems with RFC 2362, and a new specification of PIM-SM version 2 is currently being produced by the IETF. There have been many implementations of PIM-SM and it is widely used.

DVMRP: The distance vector multicast routing protocol is multicast routing protocol that takes the routing decision based upon the source address of the packet.

- This algorithm constructs the routing tree for a network.
- Whenever a router receives a packet, it forwards it to some of its ports based on the source address of packet.

The rest of the routing tree is made by downstream routers.

- In this way, routing tree is created from destination to source.
- The protocol must achieve the following tasks:

1. It must prevent the formation of loops in the network.
2. It must prevent the formation of duplicate packets.
3. It must ensure that the path traveled by a packet is the shortest from its source to the router.
4. It should provide dynamic membership.

To accomplish this, the DVMR algorithm uses a process based on following decision making strategies:

1. Reverse Path Forwarding (RPF)

- In this strategy, the router only forwards those packets that have traveled the shortest path from source to destination.
- To achieve this, the router pretends that it has a packet to send to the source from where the packet has arrived.
- In this way, the shortest path to the sender of the packet is computed.
- If the same route is followed by the received packet, it is forwarded to the next router and it is discarded otherwise.
- The reverse path forwarding ensures that the network receives a copy of the packet without formation of loops. A loop occurs when a packet that has left the router may come back again from another interface or the same interface and be forwarded again.
- RPF does not guarantee that there would be no duplicate packets in the network i.e. the network may receive two or more copies. The reason for this is that the routing is based on the source address and not on the destination address.

2. Reverse Path Broadcasting (RPB)

- In order to solve the problem, RPB is used.

• In this method, one parent router is defined for each network.

• The network could accept the multicast packets from this parent router only.

• This router sends packets to those ports for which it is designated as parent. Thus, RPB principle' allows a router to broadcast the packet in the network.

This creates duplicate packets on the network and reduces the network efficiency.

3. Reverse Path Multicasting (RPM)

• To overcome the problem of broadcasting in RPB, Reverse Path Multicasting in used.

• In this the desired multicast network tree is created by using two different methods: Pruning and grafting.

• A router can send a prune message to its upstream router whenever it finds that its network is not interested in a multicast packet. In this way a router prunes (cuts) its network from multicasting.

• If a router receives prune message from all the downstream routers, it in turn, sends a prune message to its upstream router.

• A router can also send a graft message to its upstream router if it finds that its network is again interested in receiving the multicast packet. In this way, graft message forces the upstream router to resume sending the multicast message. The network is again grafted (joined).

4. Multicast Open Shortest Path First (MOSPF)

• Multicast open shortest path first is the multicast version of open shortest path first protocol.

• It is an extension of OSPF that uses multicast link state routing method to create source based trees.

• The method used by MOSPF is different from DVMRP.

• The first difference is· that in this method, the tree is least cost tree instead of shortest path tree.

• The second .difference is that the tree is not made gradually. It is made immediately it is prepruned and ready to use.

www.ingramcontent.com/pod-product-compliance
Ingram Content Group UK Ltd.
Pitfield, Milton Keynes, MK11 3LW, UK
UKHW022022190726
13853UKWH00005B/2057